Contents

access to history

in depth

VOTES
for WOMEN
1860–1928

Paula Bartley

Hodder & Stoughton

A MEMBER OF THE HODDER HEADLINE GROUP

The poster on the front cover is reproduced courtesy of the London Museum.

Dedication: For Kate McNaughton

Order queries: please contact Bookpoint Ltd, 39 Milton Park, Abingdon, Oxon OX14 4TD. Telephone: (44) 01235 400414, Fax (44) 01235 400454. Lines are open from 9.00 - 6.00, Monday to Saturday, with a 24 hour message answering service. Email address: orders@bookpoint.co.uk

British Library Cataloguing in Publication Data

A catalogue for this title is available form the British Library

ISBN 0-340-69724-5

First published 1998

Impression number	10	9	8	7	6	5
Year			2002	2001	2000	

Illustrations by Ian Foulis & Associates Ltd, Saltash
Typeset by Sempringham publishing services, Bedford
Printed in Great Britain for Hodder & Stoughton educational, a division of Hodder Headline Plc, 338 Euston Road, London NW1 3BH
by Redwood Books, Trowbridge, Wiltshire

Preface

The original *Access to History* series was conceived as a collection of sets of books covering popular chronological periods in British history, such as 'The Tudors' and 'the nineteenth century', together with the histories of other countries, such as France, Germany, Russia and the USA. This arrangement complemented the way in which early-modern and modern history has traditionally been taught in sixth forms, colleges and universities. In recent years, however, other ways of dividing up the past have become increasingly popular. In particular, there has been a greater emphasis on studying relatively brief periods in considerable detail and on comparing similar historical phenomena in different countries. These developments have generated a demand for appropriate learning materials, and, in response, two new 'strands' are being added to the main series - *In Depth and Themes*. The new volumes build directly on the features that have made *Access to History* so popular.

To the general reader

Although *Access* books have been specifically designed to meet the needs of examination students, these volumes also have much to offer the general reader. Access authors are committed to the belief that good history must not only be accurate, up-to-date and scholarly, but also clearly and attractively written. The main body of the text (excluding the Study Guides) should, therefore, form a readable and engaging survey of a topic. Moreover, each author has aimed not merely to provide as clear an explanation as possible of what happened in the past but also to stimulate readers and to challenge them into thinking for themselves about the past and its significance. Thus, although no prior knowledge is expected from the reader, he or she is treated as an intelligent and thinking person throughout. The author tends to share ideas and explore possibilities, instead of delivering so-called 'historical truths' from on high.

To the student reader

It is intended that *Access* books should be used by students studying History at a higher level. Its volumes are all designed to be working texts, which should be reasonably clear on a first reading but which will benefit from re-reading and close study. To be an effective and successful student, you need to budget your time wisely. Hence you should think carefully about how important the material in a particular book is for you. If you simply need to acquire a general grasp of a topic, the following approach will probably be effective:

1 Read Chapter 1, which should give you an overview of the whole book, and think about its contents.

2 Skim through Chapter 2, paying particular attention to the opening section and to the headings and sub-headings. Decide if you need to read the whole chapter.
3 If you do, read the chapter, stopping at the end of every sub-division of the text to make notes.
4 Repeat stage 2 (and stage 3 where appropriate) for the other chapters.

If, however, your course - and your particular approach to it - demands a detailed knowledge of the contents of the book, you will need to be correspondingly more thorough. There is no perfect way of studying, and it is particularly worthwhile experimenting with different styles of note-making to find the one that best suits you. Nevertheless, the following plan of action is worth trying:

1 Read a whole chapter quickly, preferably at one sitting. Avoid the temptation - which may be very great - to make notes at this stage.
2 Study the flow diagram at the end of the chapter, ensuring that you understand the general 'shape' of what you have read.
3 Re-read the chapter more slowly, this time taking notes. You may well be amazed at how much more intelligible and straightforward the material seems on a second reading - and your notes will be correspondingly more useful to you when you have to write an essay or revise for an exam. In the long run, reading a chapter twice can, in fact, often save time. Be sure to make your notes in a clear, orderly fashion, and spread them out so that, if necessary, you can later add extra information.
4 Read the advice on essay questions, and do tackle the specimen titles. (Remember that if learning is to be effective, it must be active. No one - alas - has yet devised any substitute for real effort. It is up to you to make up your own mind on the key issues in any topic.)
5 Attempt the source-based questions. The guidance on tackling these exercises, which is generally given at least once in a book, is well worth reading and thinking about.

When you have finished the main chapters, go through the 'Further Reading' section. Remember that no single book can ever do more than introduce a topic, and it is to be hoped that - time permitting - you will want to read more widely. If *Access* books help you to discover just how diverse and fascinating the human past can be, the series will have succeeded in its aim - and you will experience that enthusiasm for the subject which, along with efficient learning, is the hallmark of all the best students.

Robert Pearce

1 Introduction: Change and Continuity in the Position of Women 1860-1918

'Watch out, boys - they're coming. From now on, the House of Commons will no longer be a men-only club.'[1] So predicted a leading article when 116 women won seats as MPs in the 1997 general election, 79 years after women were first granted the vote. However, in 1918 the majority of women were still denied the franchise as the vote was only given to women over the age of 30 who were on the local government register or married to men on the local government register. In fact, women had to wait another ten years before they achieved the vote on equal terms with men. Eventually, in 1928, all women, regardless of their marital status or financial position, were enfranchised. Even so, votes for women were gained only after a long, and at times highly controversial, campaign. This book tells the story of the suffragists (usually thought of as peaceful campaigners) and the suffragettes (usually thought of as more violent) who fought hard for this objective. Yet, although this book is about women's suffrage, the vote was just one of a number of demands put forward by those who campaigned for social change. By the time women had gained even a limited vote, early feminists (that is women who wanted to improve the position of women) had chalked up some formidable achievements.

1 Education

Education was seen, by feminists, as the key to unlock the closed doors of the masculine world of politics. In the 1860s when the campaign for the suffrage began in earnest, the majority of women from all social classes generally lacked a formal education, but by 1918 there had been some remarkable changes, though not all as a response to pressure from women and not always beneficial to them. As Dorothy Thomson has pointed out, generalizations about a whole gender have to be treated with great caution'.[2] Educational developments affected working-class and middle-class girls and women quite differently: while it is thought to have limited the working class, it opened up opportunities for their middle-class counterparts.

Until 1870 working-class girls were educated in a variety of ways. Young factory workers attended factory schools, whereas pauper children went to workhouse schools. The remainder of the female population, if formally educated at all, were taught in small fee-paying schools run by older women or charity schools set up by religious foundations. After 1870 state schools replaced this informal system. The period from 1870 onwards saw the construction of a state education system which by 1918 had made schooling compulsory for all children up to the age of thirteen. The new state-funded system of education gave some chances for working-class girls to become numerate and literate - by the end of the nineteenth century 97 per cent of all children could read and write - but it offered too narrow a curriculum, too rigid a teaching method and too large a class size to have any great effect. State schools emphasised the domestication, rather than the emancipation, of working-class girls. All too often, the school syllabus included cookery, needlework and housewifery at the expense of other subjects. Indeed, in 1878, domestic economy became a compulsory subject for girls but not for boys. It has been suggested that state schools were more finishing schools for the manual worker, preparing girls either for domestic service or for the role of wife and mother, rather than educational establishments in the wider sense. In this way they reaffirmed, rather than challenged, women's role in society. Change, for the young working-class school girl, did not therefore necessarily mean progress.

In contrast, the changes in middle-class education occurred as a result of pressure from below and, possibly as a consequence of this, offered better opportunities. In mid-nineteenth century Britain the majority of girls of the middle and upper classes did not go to school but were educated at home by a governess or by a member of their family. Some attended small family-type schools but the nature of their education remained virtually identical to that of those taught at home. Middle-class and upper-class girls were educated to be wives and mothers of men from the same social class rather than to go out to work for a living. By 1918, largely through the combined efforts of feminists and the government, this had changed to some extent because a number of new schools, which offered an academic curriculum consisting of science, economics and mathematics, were opened for the daughters of middle- and upper-class families.

Feminists also worked hard to achieve entry to higher education for women. By 1860 both Queen's and Bedford College, London had educated a number of leading feminists such as Barbara Bodichon and Elizabeth Blackwell yet the rest of higher education remained resolutely male. All women, whatever their intelligence or capability, were denied access to both universities and medical schools. This prompted a number of feminists to campaign for women's access to medical training and universities and to promote the training of teachers. By the end of the nineteenth century both London and Manchester Universities accepted women, various women's colleges had been founded at Oxford and Cambridge (even though women were not allowed to be awarded degrees) and women's teacher training colleges established. In turn these women went to teach in the newly opened secondary schools for girls. However, despite the opening of a Working Women's College in London in the 1860s, opportunities for working-class women remained limited. Furthermore, with an increasing emphasis placed on teacher training, the old pupil-teacher scheme (whereby bright working-class girls learnt to become teachers by working in a classroom alongside a fully qualified professional) fell into disrepute and subsequently came to a close.

2 Work

As with education, there were great differences between middle-class and working-class working patterns. Indeed, there were two labour markets for women in this period: one for working-class women and another for the middle class. Despite ongoing technological change, and apart from a brief interlude during the First World War, domestic service continued to be the most common occupation for working-class women. Apparently one in three working-class women were domestic servants at some time in their lives.

Cotton remained Britain's most important export throughout this time, so it is not surprising that textile work remained the second most important job for women. However, this work was concentrated in the cotton towns of northern England and in parts of Scotland rather than spread throughout the British Isles. Elsewhere, women were employed in a variety of unskilled and low paid jobs. Yet, there were a number of new developments. As a result of the growth of banking and commerce, combined with the subsequent inventions of the typewriter and the telephone, new opportunities were created for the 'white blouse' worker as she was known.

Nevertheless, despite a number of trade union and government attempts to improve wages, and working conditions, working-class women remained at the bottom of the economic scale. Certainly by 1914, working hours had been reduced, minimum wages had been set in four trades and in some areas - such as laundries - working conditions had improved as a result of legislation. However, equality with men was a long way off as most women workers continued to earn about 65 per cent of a male wage.

On the other hand, when this book begins, it was expected that middle-class women - single or married - should remain at home, look after their families and engage in charitable works. If they were forced to work for payment, as many were, the occupation of governess was open to them. By 1914, however, middle-class women had created new professions and had made a few inroads into a number of previously male dominated ones. A School for Nursing, for instance, was established at St Thomas's Hospital, London, in 1860 by Florence Nightingale which attracted middle-class women. Women also gained the right to become doctors, architects, factory and workhouse inspectors and to enter the civil service. By far the greatest number, however, became teachers. Even so, there were still a number of professions, such as the law, banking and the stock exchange, which remained closed to women. Until the First World War, the sexual division of labour, whereby women and men were designated to do different jobs, remained almost insuperable. During this war, which lasted from 1914 to 1918, the nature of women's work altered dramatically but this did not last as most women returned to their traditional jobs when the war ended.

3 Marriage

Largely as a result of feminist pressure, Parliament was persuaded to make a number of significant changes in the legal position of both working-class and middle-class married women in the nineteenth and early twentieth centuries. When the suffrage movement began, women very much remained the unequal partner in marriage, so not surprisingly feminists of the time campaigned to end a number of the grosser legal injustices. Some of the areas of concern centred on property rights, marital rights, custody of children and divorce. For example, once married, women were considered the property of their husbands and had few legal rights. Husbands owned the home and the wealth of their wives, whether or not they were still living together. In the notorious case of the Norton family, George Norton took all the money earned by his wife Caroline after they had separated. On the other hand, husbands were responsible for their wives' debts and so, in return, Caroline Norton ran up bills which her husband was forced to pay. After considerable campaigning by feminists - such as the suffragist and suffragette Elizabeth Wolstenholme Elmy - the Married Women's Property Acts of 1870 and 1882 gave, if not equal status to women, then a stepping stone to future reform.

A number of feminists also expressed concern about the high incidence of wife-battering and rape in marriage. The Matrimonial Causes Act in 1884 went some way towards ending marital injustice by denying husbands the right to confine wives who refused to have sex with them. In 1891 this Act was reinforced by the Court of Appeals' decision on the Jackson marriage case. Soon after marriage Mr Jackson went to New Zealand to set up a business but a year later, at the request of his wife, he returned - but his wife refused to see him. In response, Mr Jackson, helped by two accomplices, grabbed her outside her church in Clitheroe, forced her into his carriage, took her to his home and locked her up. Fortunately for Mrs Jackson, her friends led a campaign for her release and after a long legal struggle the Court of Appeal decided that Mr Jackson had no statutory right to force his wife to live with him. Nevertheless, Mrs Jackson suffered from considerable hostility from the people in her home town for refusing to live with her husband. Furthermore, despite the work of feminists, wife-battering and marital rape remained legal.

Divorce law exhibited similar inequalities. Before 1867 it was extremely difficult and very expensive to obtain a divorce in England. Only very rich - and determined - men were generally able to afford the high costs of divorce. The 1867 Divorce Act reformed the divorce law but it benefited men rather than women. Men were able to divorce their wives for adultery, whereas women had to prove either bigamy, rape, sodomy, bestiality, cruelty or long-term desertion to gain a divorce. This, argued nineteenth century feminists, consolidated the sexual double standard (the moral standard whereby it was acceptable for men, but not women, to have sex outside marriage) because it laid down different grounds for divorce. Moreover, once divorced, women found it difficult to obtain maintenance and custody of their children. There were some improvements in the 1870s and 1880s when wives who had been beaten or deserted by their husbands were granted maintenance and divorced women were given some custody rights over their children. Nevertheless marital equality with men was not achieved by the time women won the vote.

4 Sexual Morality

This period, according to Sheila Jeffreys, also 'witnessed a massive campaign by women to transform male sexual behaviour and protect women from the effects of the exercise of a form of male sexuality damaging to their interests'.[3] In particular, feminists expressed concern about the sexual double standard. One of their greatest victories was the repeal of the Contagious Diseases Acts (CDAs) in 1886. These Acts, the first of which had been passed in 1864, allowed police in a number of garrison towns and naval ports the right to arrest women suspected of being common prostitutes and require them to be medically examined for venereal disease. If found infected, women could be detained for treatment. This, according to feminists, was unfair because it blamed prostitutes for the spread of venereal disease not the men who used their services. Under the leadership of Josephine Butler, the Ladies' National Association led a campaign to repeal these Acts and eventually succeeded 22 years after they had been passed.

The success of this campaign prompted feminists to launch a crusade against the sexual exploitation of young girls. In 1885 they achieved a victory when the Criminal Law Amendment Act, which raised the age of sexual consent to 16, was passed. Feminists and others founded The National Vigilance Association to ensure that this Act was put into practice and to promote equal high moral standards amongst the sexes. Edwardian feminists, such as Christabel Pankhurst, took up the social purity cause and demanded that men improve their moral code by remaining chaste outside marriage. Although feminists achieved a small victory in repealing the CDAs, the campaign to raise moral standards can be considered to have failed miserably.

5 Politics

Women may not have achieved the British Parliamentary vote until 1918 but there were other political achievements. On January 1st 1881, 700 British women were able to vote at the House of Keys in the Isle of Man, 37 years before women in mainland Britain were granted the same privilege. The Manx, as the people who live in the Isle of Man were known, had kept their own institutions, independent of Britain, and governed themselves through the Tynwald Court, which had an Upper Chamber and an elected House of Keys.

Elsewhere in Britain, women were engaged in politics through their party organisations. The Women's Liberal Federation, which was founded in 1886, was an autonomous, women-only organisation which offered invaluable training to feminists. Delegates at Annual meetings claimed the right to define party policy and concerned themselves with suffrage and with radical social policies, such as health, housing and education. Similarly the Independent Labour Party, founded in 1893, attracted large numbers of women activists who spoke at meetings, wrote articles in newspapers and helped develop party policy. Women also joined the women's section of the Conservative Party but tended to play more of a secondary role than their Liberal and Labour counterparts.

It is sometimes forgotten that some women achieved the vote in local government long before they won the right to vote in national elections. In 1869 single or widowed rate-paying women were given the right to vote for municipal councils and the later county councils; in 1907 all women rate-payers were allowed to vote in local government elections. Middle-class women in London's poorest areas 'worked all hours to get property repaired and fumigated, drains rebuilt, infant mortality reduced, and open spaces inserted into the slums'.[4] Women also encouraged authorities to build public lavatories, baths and parks for the inhabitants of working-class districts. However, after the Liberals swept into power in 1906 electors began to vote Tory in town councils and so large numbers of women - who tended to be left-wing - lost their seats.

In 1870, as a result of the Education Act, women were eligible to serve on the newly created School Boards which had responsibility for the education of children in state schools from the age of five upwards. Some women sought election because they wanted to make a public statement that women were capable of governing. Others, such as the suffragist Lydia Becker, tried to put their feminist ideas into practice by encouraging boys as well as girls to do cooking and needlework. This work was not to last. When Local Education Authorities replaced School Boards in 1902 women were declared ineligible for election.

The Liberal Party encouraged women to serve as Poor Law Guardians because the skills and competencies they offered would demonstrate their fitness for the vote. In 1875 the first women Poor Law Guardian was elected and by 1900 there were approximately 1,000 women Guardians, many of whom, like Emmeline Pankhurst, tried to mitigate the worst excesses of workhouse life. As a Poor Law Guardian in Manchester, she found

1 old folks sitting on backless forms or benches. They had no privacy, no possessions, not even a locker. The old women were without pockets in their gowns so they were obliged to keep any poor little treasures they had in their bosoms. Soon after I took office we gave
5 the old people comfortable Windsor chairs to sit in, and in a number of ways we managed to make their existence more endurable.[5]

Agatha Stacey, a Birmingham Poor Law Guardian, was so concerned about the 'deserving' poor in the local workhouse that she helped to found homes for the homeless, single mothers and the mentally retarded. A number of female Poor Law Guardians were prominent figures in Poor Law administration nationally and used their influence to initiate reforms elsewhere.

Women who campaigned for social change faced heavy criticism because they criticised the 'separate spheres' philosophy which dominated this period. According to Victorian and Edwardian sentiment, God made men and women biologically different so it made sense that they performed distinct roles. Women were the only sex able to become pregnant, have babies and breast-feed, so it was thought appropriate for them to remain within the 'private sphere' of the home. Not surprisingly, women were also believed to be better qualified for the domestic jobs of cooking, cleaning and child-rearing because home was their natural domain. In contrast, men's historic hunting role made them innately suited for the 'public sphere' of work and politics. In claiming a share of the 'public sphere' for women, feminists therefore challenged the fundamental principles of society.

During the period 1860 to 1918, women experienced a number of significant improvements to their lives. However, despite some success in changing the position of women for the better, enough inequality remained for the suffragists and the suffragettes to want to eradicate it. And so, by the time Edward VII became King in 1901, the vote had become their major focus of attention.

References

1   Fran Abrams, *The Independent,* May 3rd 1997, p. 8.
2   Dorothy Thompson in Jane Rendall's *Equal or Different* (Basil Blackwell, 1987), p. 71.
3   Sheila Jeffreys, *The Spinster and her Enemies* (Pandora, 1985), p. 1.
4   Patricia Hollis in Jane Rendall's *Equal or Different* , p. 204.
5   Emmeline Pankhurst, *My Own Story* (Virago, 1979), p. 24.

Making notes on 'Introduction: Change and Continuity in the Position of Women 1860-1918'

There is no one correct way to make notes. Some students prefer to make notes in a conventional linear way and write down a list of the main points of each chapter. Others like to experiment and make charts and diagrams. If you prefer to take linear notes the following structure will help you:

1.   Working-class women and work.
      (i)   type of work
a)   domestic service
b)   cotton
c)   new opportunities
      (ii) characterised by low pay and poor conditions
2.   Middle class women and work.
      (i)   excluded from work force
      (ii) professionalisation of middle-class women
Conclusion: sexual division of labour until the First World War.

The summary diagrams which are provided in each chapter provide a basis for those who prefer to make charts and diagrams.

Summary Diagram

Introduction: Change and Continuity in the Position of Women 1860-1918

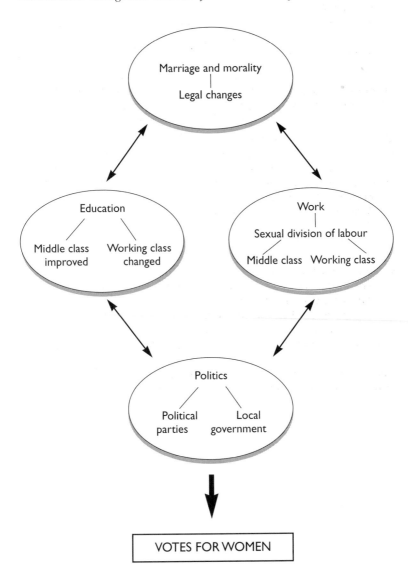

2 Votes for Women: The Debate

Initially the vote had been seen by voters as an obligation, like paying taxes, rather than a human right. By the mid-nineteenth century, however, the vote had gained a symbolic significance for some women, who believed that its absence reflected their second-class status. Not surprisingly, given the broad political composition of the suffrage movement, there emerged several different arguments in support of votes for women. Historians have viewed these arguments in a number of ways. Constitutional historians tend to stress the political reasons why women sought the vote; socialist feminists tend to emphasise the economic causes; and radical feminists tend to concentrate on the importance of sexual politics. However, some of the latest research suggests that beliefs in British, and sometimes white, superiority underpinned the women's suffrage campaign. Fears were certainly expressed that black men were gaining the vote elsewhere whereas white women were still excluded. Those who opposed women's suffrage marshalled equally numerous arguments against votes for women. Until recently historians have generally ignored this opposition movement possibly because it was considered unfashionable - and perhaps politically incorrect - to examine those who were hostile to what was considered a reasonable demand.

1 The Case for Votes for Women

a) The Rights of Women

Historians agree that early suffragists claimed what they believed to be the restoration of an old right rather than the exercise of a new privilege. Suffragists claimed that women had in the past played a significant role in parliamentary politics and drew on many historical examples to support this argument. Abbesses who owned vast tracts of land in the medieval period had attended and participated in the early Parliaments. In particular, the abbesses of Barking and Winchester, who headed two of the most prestigious abbeys in medieval England, had been involved in policy making at the highest level. Even when the English Reformation, by the closure of the abbeys and convents, put paid to religious women's involvement in Parliamentary affairs, lay women allegedly continued to influence politics. In the sixteenth century, it was argued, women freeholders were still able to vote at parliamentary elections. In 1867 large numbers of women householders re-claimed this old privilege for themselves and tried to register but, though many had successfully placed themselves on the electoral roll, most were rejected. This led to an appeal in the Court of Common Pleas where over 5,000 Manchester women, defended by Richard Pankhurst, claimed the right to vote. The judges disagreed

THE DIGNITY OF THE FRANCHISE.

QUALIFIED VOTER. "AH, YOU MAY PAY RATES AN' TAXES, AN' YOU MAY 'AVE RESPONSERBILITH
ALL; BUT WHEN IT COMES TO *VOTIN'*, YOU MUST LEAVE IT TO *US MEN!*"

Punch *cartoon reproduced by the Women's Social and Political Union (WSPU)*

with this claim and held that 'every woman is personally incapable' of voting. And so, after 1868, because the suffragists lost the legal case for women's suffrage, the argument that women were legally entitled to vote also lost its persuasive appeal.

Since manhood suffrage was based on property qualifications, both suffragists and suffragettes thought it particularly inequitable that women were denied the vote. This argument gained considerable ground after each extension of the franchise gave the vote to more and more men on the basis of property. When the property qualification for the male vote was lowered in 1867 and again in 1884, more and more wealthy women saw men less wealthy than themselves obtain the vote. Although women owned and controlled vast acres of land, enjoyed fortunes derived from industry and were both house-holders and taxpayers, they did not have equal privileges with men of their class as they were unable to take part in the increasingly democratic process. After 1884 30,000 Englishwomen farmers watched many of their male agricultural workers use their newly acquired vote while they remained disenfranchised. It was therefore argued that as women were permitted to hold property, they should be permitted to exercise the political rights that possession of property brought to its holder. The cartoon shown on page 11 illustrates this well. It was first produced by *Punch*, a satirical magazine, but was later used by the WSPU as propaganda in support of votes for women. The man entering the polling station is obviously working-class and is portrayed, by both his physical appearance, his body language and his speech, as inferior to the upright, respectable and middle-class woman left outside. It therefore confirms the women's suffrage argument that illiterate and uneducated men were enfranchised, and probably shouldn't have been, whereas educated and literate women were excluded, and should have been enfranchised. Furthermore, taxation and representation were seen to be inextricably linked in the British parliamentary system as it was held that those who put money into the national purse should be able to control its spending. Suffragists and suffragettes were annoyed that even when women paid taxes they had no control over how those taxes were spent.

Historians have frequently seen women's claim for the vote as the last in a set of other economic, social and political rights. David Morgan, for example, places the campaign for the vote within the wider context of female emancipation in general. By the end of the nineteenth century, Morgan argues, women had obtained most of the benefits that a political democracy could afford: they enjoyed improved educational opportunities; had effected considerable legal changes; were permeating the technological and professional labour market; and were increasingly joining trade unions to campaign for their economic rights. Certainly, suffragists drew attention to the increasing gap between women's economic participation and their continual absence from the political sphere. However, it is important to remember that the campaigns for the vote took place at the same time, rather than after, the campaigns for legal changes and other rights. In addition, as the introduction to this book has demonstrated, success in these areas was limited. The campaign for the vote should therefore be seen as part and parcel of the women's movement of the nineteenth and early twentieth centuries not just the last emancipatory hurdle to be overcome.

b) Growth of Democracy

The vote is also seen by historians to have had an important symbolic significance, as it was considered to be the hallmark of citizenship in every country which was governed by a representative institution. Suffragists were therefore thought to be particularly disheartened when women were consistently omitted from each of the franchise reform Acts of 1832, 1867 and 1884 and were thus denied the badge of citizenship. The Great Reform Act of 1832 swept away many of the abuses of the Parliamentary system but the new vote was to be confined to men of property. Suffragists argued that, for the first time in legal and political history, women were explicitly excluded from participating in the democratic process because the Act had deliberately used the term 'male' rather than 'persons'. The attainment of household suffrage in the boroughs in 1867 threw the exclusion of women from the democratic process into even sharper relief. Although not all men were enfranchised - the residence qualification meant that domestic servants, the armed forces and sons living at home were still excluded - many were. By 1884 two-thirds of adult males had gained the vote, but all women, like criminals and patients in lunatic asylums, were denied the vote. Suffragists considered it inappropriate to claim that Britain had a representative government when the majority of the population was disenfranchised on the grounds of gender. By the end of the nineteenth century they even claimed that Britain had an unjust and unbalanced political system.

The successful participation of a small number of women in both party and local politics reinforced women's claim to the parliamentary vote. The three franchise reform Acts of the nineteenth century, combined with the secret ballot of 1872 and the Corrupt Practices Act of 1883 (which limited the use of paid canvassers), created a need for sophisticated party machines to organise the new mass electorate. Various women's organisations were set up within the main parties with the dual purpose of shaping women's opinion and canvassing votes. Women also made a significant contribution to local politics and to philanthropy. The accomplishments of women in party and local politics made it abundantly clear to suffragists that they were fit to be entrusted with the vote. It was also considered unfair that a few distinguished women, who had already made a significant contribution to the country's good, should be disenfranchised whereas illiterate and uneducated men had already obtained the vote. Women such as Louisa Twining (workhouse reformer) and Angela Burdett-Coutts (famous rich philanthropist) and Florence Nightingale (nursing reformer) were cited by suffragists as examples of women who had advanced the cause of reform politics and who would contribute much of value - for both men and women - to future parliaments.

c) Means to an End

Of course, it was not just the vote as a symbol of citizenship which mattered but the use to which it could be put. At the beginning of the nineteenth century the vote had been less significant than patronage in Parliamentary politics and, with so many of the population denied the vote, it had little real influence on government thinking. However, historians suggest that by the end of the nineteenth century women involved in philanthropic and social work viewed the vote as a powerful tool to transform the lives of their sex. Suffragists and suffragettes believed that under a representative government, the interests of any non-represented group were liable to be neglected. The group which held political power, that was men, made laws favourable to themselves and neglected the interests of those without power, including women. This reasoning was borne out by experience: as more and more men were enfranchised, so laws were enacted which reflected the wishes of the various classes of male voter. After 1832 the Whigs passed a series of laws including the Poor Law Amendment Act (1834) which represented the particular interests of the newly enfranchised middle class, whereas after 1867, when working-class men were granted the vote, important educational and trade union reforms were introduced. In contrast, it was believed that women faced hardship because their views remained unrepresented. Indeed the male electorate was seen to use their sole power to make laws, such as the Contagious Diseases Acts, (see page 5) which adversely affected, and were strongly resented by, women. Moreover, whereas early Victorian governments adhered much more to the principle of *laissez faire*, it was apparent by the Edwardian era that this principle was dead and that Parliament, as the governing body of the country, had the authority to change the way people worked and lived.

Once women had obtained the vote, suffragists and suffragettes argued, governments would be forced to take women's issues seriously. Both groups considered the vote to be a defence against the tyranny of men over women and believed that when women were enfranchised their oppression would end. But even though the vote was seen as a means to the end of greater social justice, that end varied considerably. For some it meant economic reform and the improvement of women's financial situation, for some legal reform and the improvement of women's marital position and for another group social reform and the improvement of women's condition more generally.

Socialist feminist historians such as Liddington and Norris tend to focus on the fact that suffragists wanted the vote to improve the pay, conditions and lives of working women. In 1872 suffragists alleged that, in England alone, nearly three million unmarried women and 800,000 married women received wages far below those of men of the same class. Forty years later, suffragettes were making similar observations. In 1912 it was believed that male working-class wages had risen throughout the late nineteenth and early twentieth centuries because men were able, through their trade unions, to pressurise Parliament into passing laws favourable to them. In contrast, it was believed that women's trade unions accomplished less, largely because they were without the vote. Women not only earned less than half the male wage but were barred from a number of occupations. Throughout the nineteenth century governments had excluded women from certain types of work, restricted their hours and regulated their working conditions. For example, women had been banned from working underground in coal mines in 1842 and in 1844 had their hours restricted in textile factories. Many suffragists objected to this 'protective' legislation because it either deprived women of jobs or made them compete unfairly with men for work, resulting in the further lowering of female wages and, paradoxically, women being dismissed in favour of men. In the Edwardian period, suffragettes put forward similar arguments and believed that the vote would help to bring about economic equality between men and women.

Throughout the nineteenth century suffragists wanted the vote as a legal protection against avaricious and cruel husbands. Before the Married Women's Property Acts were passed (1870 and 1882) the common law deprived women of the right to keep their own property and money. Even after 1882 the British marriage laws were considered the most barbarous in Europe as husbands still had the right to beat their wives and compel them to return if they left home. Children over seven were legally the property of their fathers, who were able to remove them from their mothers if they wished. By the beginning of the twentieth century, when many of the principal legal injustices had been removed, both suffragists and suffragettes turned to issues of sex and morality.

Until the recent work of feminist historians most history texts ignored the emphasis placed on sex and morality by the suffragists and suffragettes. The few historians who do mention it have often used it as an excuse to ridicule the suffragettes. In particular, George Dangerfield and Roger Fulford both dismiss the WSPU's cry for 'Votes for Women' and 'Chastity for Men' as an amusing peculiarity while Rosen discounts these slogans as a spinsterish eccentricity. However, the relationship between sexuality and the vote has enjoyed a long history in the annals of women's suffrage. Both the suffragists and the suffragettes positioned women's franchise within the wider context of sexual politics and took the question of sexuality very earnestly indeed. For some suffrage campaigners such as Millicent Fawcett and Christabel Pankhurst the vote was as much a tool for improving men's sexual morality as it was for improving women's working conditions.

Although the majority of suffragists remained opposed to debates about female sexuality, fearing that it would offend Victorian prudery and so lessen support, a number wanted the vote to cleanse the perceived corruption of public life, ensuring that men and women adhered to the same moral principles. This, in turn, would go some way towards eliminating venereal disease. The women's suffrage movement was therefore seen as much as a moral movement as a political one. Indeed, some suffragists believed in a female moral superiority, whereby women were the keepers of virtue and men the lustful destroyers of chastity. Lydia Becker, one of the founders of the suffragist movement, insisted that the vote was 'a protection for women from the uncontrolled dominion of the savage passions of men.' Over thirty years later, Emmeline Pankhurst confidently assumed that votes for women were necessary to eliminate the sexual double standard whereby it was acceptable for men, but not women, to engage in pre-marital sex. When Emmeline Pankhurst was a Poor Law Guardian she had been distressed by the increasing number of single mothers who were dependent on the state because men refused to marry them or pay them maintenance. Christabel Pankhurst even claimed that venereal disease (she claimed 75 per cent of men were infected with gonorrhea and 25 per cent with syphilis!) would be eliminated once women had the vote. In her pamphlet *The Great Scourge* she argued that the subjection of women was the fundamental cause of venereal disease and promoted a two-fold political programme of chastity for men and votes for women. Indeed, she fervently believed that once women were enfranchised laws could be passed to transform male sexual behaviour:

1 the canker of venereal disease is eating away the vitals of the nation, and the only cure is Votes for Women. ... The real cure of the great plague is - Votes for Women, which will give to women more self-reliance and a stronger economic position and chastity for men ...

5 Apart from the deplorable moral effect of the fact that women are voteless, there is this to be noticed - that the law of the land, as made and administered by men, protects and encourages the immorality of men, and the sex exploitation of women.[1]

This extract from her pamphlet, which might read a little strangely to modern eyes, needs to be placed within historical context. Both Victorian and Edwardian Britain was anxious about the increase of venereal disease and its far reaching effects not only on the health of the individual but on that of the nation. Nevertheless, it is fair to assume that Christabel Pankhurst cherished too many assumptions about the superiority of female virtue and expressed a minority view when she associated venereal disease with votes for women.

The vote was also seen as a device which could be utilised to curb unfair legislation against prostitutes and ultimately to end prostitution. In particular, Victorian suffragists were critical of the Contagious Diseases Acts (CDAs) of the 1860s because they blamed prostitutes for venereal disease, not the men who paid for their services. Feminists, under the leadership of Josephine Butler's Ladies' National Association (LNA), opposed these Acts and supported votes for women to end this legal injustice. Meanwhile, because they believed the CDAs to be so unfair, the membership of the LNA continued to campaign against them in the hope that an all-male Parliament might repeal the Acts. Some went even further. Millicent Fawcett not only supported the LNA campaigns but believed that the vote would also end prostitution. As President of both the National Union of Women's Suffrage Societies (NUWSS) and the National Union of Women Workers (an umbrella organisation initially concerned with the elimination of prostitution), Fawcett was well placed to see a direct connection between women's lack of franchise and the existence of prostitution. This link was also confirmed by a leading member of the NUWSS in the early years of the twentieth century:

1 We wish for it [the vote] because there exists a terrible trade of
   procuring young girls for immoral purposes. The girl is first
   entrapped and seduced, and when once she has fallen, it is very
   difficult for her to return afterwards to her home, or to be received
5 among respectable girls in workshops or in domestic service. She
   becomes a prostitute ... we believe the time has come when women
   must claim their right to help ... and the first step to this lies in their
   enfranchisement, for without this they have no real power in the
   matter. It would be much more difficult for this cruel and wicked
10 traffic to be carried on if it were recognised by the law that women
   were of the same value and had the same standing in the State as
   men.

The causes of prostitution were located within the economic and political context of dependency: most women did not earn enough to support themselves and relied too much on men to help them out. Christabel Pankhurst went further and argued that prostitution was based on male vice, which could only be eradicated when women had the vote.

More recent interpretations by historians such as Catherine Hall place the reasons why women wanted the vote within the context of British imperialism. It is argued that 'a sense of national and racial superiority based on Britain's imperial status was an organising principle of Victorian culture'[2] and that most feminists subscribed to the belief that the Anglo-Saxon race was superior to all others. Although (mostly Quaker) suffragists initially drew comparisons between women's rights and abolitionism by supporting the emancipation of both women and black people, by the end of the nineteenth century a number of suffragists were believed to have changed their minds. It was feared that when the black male population of the United States were enfranchised in the 1860s it sent out the racial message that black men were capable of exercising political judgement whereas the majority of the white race - that is women - were not. As a result, it was thought impolitic not to grant the vote to British women because it undermined the concept of white supremacy. Furthermore, as people of a leading colonial nation, many suffrage workers assumed Britain to be in a more advanced state of social development than the people of other countries. One argument put forward by the MP Clive Eastwick in the debate in the House of Commons on the Women's Disabilities Bill on 3rd May 1871 suggested that England, as a highly civilised country, should take the lead in educating the rest of the world:

1 There was a special reason why this country should be the first to adopt the enfranchisement of women. That reason was the immense influence which the example of England must exert upon the 200 millions of Asiatics in India, among whom, with a few brilliant
5 exceptions, women have been degraded to a state little better than slavery. How could we expect that Indian women would be emancipated from the imprisonment of the zenanah [harem] or be admitted to the full privileges of education, so long as we continued to proclaim the inferiority of women in this country?

Over 30 years later, the leadership of the WSPU reiterated this. In an editorial for *Votes for Women*, Christabel Pankhurst argued that British women were the rightful heirs to democracy and felt it disgraceful that 'they should have their inheritance withheld, while men of other races are suddenly and almost without preparation leaping into possession of constitutional power'.[3] According to one historian, both suffragists and suffragettes advocated the vote for white women over black men because Britain, as the Mother of Parliaments, provided a role model which other countries should emulate rather than the other way round. However, the emphasis on the relationship between women's suffrage, imperialism, and sometimes racism perhaps rests more on historical interpretation than actuality. Both the NUWSS and the WSPU constantly emphasised the need for women all over the world to unite in their fight for the vote with the WSPU even believing that the unity of women overrode differences in colour, race or creed.

What can be said with some degree of certainty, as the extracts from a leaflet shown opposite produced by the NUWSS in 1907 suggests, is that women wanted the vote for a number of different reasons:

Why Women Want the Vote

1   **BECAUSE** no race or class or sex can have its interest properly safeguarded in the legislature of a country unless it is represented by direct suffrage.

BECAUSE while men who are voters can get their economic
5   grievances listed to, non-voters are disregarded.

BECAUSE politics and economics go hand in hand. And so long as woman has no political status she will be the 'bottom dog' as a wage-earner.

BECAUSE the Legislature in the past has not made laws which
10   are equal between men and women: and these laws will not be altered till women get the vote.

BECAUSE all the more important and lucrative positions are barred to them, and opportunities of public service are denied.

BECAUSE wherever women have become voters, reform has
15   procceeded more rapidly than before, and even at home our munic-
ipal government, in which the women have a certain share, is in advance and not behind our Parliamentary attitude on many important questions.

BECAUSE women will be better comrades to their husbands,
20   better mothers to their children, and better housekeepers of the home.

2 The Case Against Votes for Women

To a late twentieth century audience the ideas of the opponents of women's suffrage, often called the Antis, may seem wildly unconvincing but at the time these ideas were more representative of popular opinion than those of the female suffragists. It is also important to remember that the Antis were not all men: a number of eminent women (such as Mary Kingsley and Gertrude Bell, distinguished Victorian and Edwardian explorers) spoke out against votes for women. The Antis' arguments were varied but generally centred on the perceived physical, emotional and intellectual differences between men and women.

a) The Right to Rule

As Brian Harrison has pointed out, those opposed to votes for women were often people with an inbuilt dislike of change and with no wish to alter the political status quo. To their minds, any extension of the franchise, either male or female, would have deleterious effects on the country because it would destabilise the existing political structure. A few Antis were opposed to any increase in democracy because they feared that an 'uneducated, politically inexperienced and irrational class'[4] would gain ascendancy over the body politic and this was too great a risk to take. Indeed, opponents of women's suffrage believed that a small political elite (themselves) were destined to and should rule over the mass of the population. For a lot of Antis it was self-evident that women should not vote simply because they were women. At first, Harrison argues, the inferiority of women seemed so obvious that it needed no further explanation, but gradually the Antis claimed an intellectual basis for their views.

Many Antis stressed the relationship between the right to vote and the responsibility to fight for one's country. Women, it was alleged, were not capable of full citizenship because they were not available for purposes of defence. One female leading anti-suffragist argued that women should not have the vote because political power, exercised either overseas or domestically, rested in the end on physical force to which women, owing to physical, moral and social reasons, were not capable of contributing. This argument against votes for women remained remarkably consistent between 1860 and 1914 but was one which had several strands. The first strand rested on Britain's role as an imperial power. Antis argued that as Britons ruled a vast empire they needed a strong army. No country with imperial pretensions offered female suffrage, it was said, because women could not fight to defend their country. Because women could never fulfil this vital obligation of citizenship, they should be denied the right to vote. In addition many believed that countries, such as India, over which Britain ruled would not give British authority the same respect if she was ruled by women (the fact that Queen Victoria was head of state seemed not to bother them). It was also feared that colonised countries would demand their own enfranchisement, which would inevitably lead to demands for independence, if British women received the vote. The second strand rested on fears that women's enfranchisement would introduce a new era of pacifism, as women would be reluctant to wage wars against foreign enemies. As a consequence Britain might face decline and invasion because women generally favoured peace rather than fighting. Concern was particularly expressed that the ever strengthening economic and military position of a masculinised Germany would quickly subdue the increasingly femininised Britain should there ever be a declaration of war. The third strand rested on the belief that domestic political power was equated with armed strength. It was thought that women would be unable to govern because of their inability to enforce the laws they had made; this would inevitably lead to anarchy, a brutal civil war and ultimately the end of British civilisation.

b) Psychological Differences

Men and women were perceived, by the Antis, as very different from each other not only physically but also psychologically and intellectually. Victorian scientific theory legitimised this belief by suggesting that the differences rested on a biological basis. Women were seen to be intellectually inferior to men because their brain weighed less than men's. Moreover, medical opinion claimed that women were guided by their womb - which was seen to be particularly unstable at puberty, menstruation, pregnancy and menopause - rather than their brain and thus more prone to insanity. 'The point of hysterical emotion and unreason is always nearer with women ... their nerve force is slighter, their self-restraint less.'[5] Indeed the word hysteria is derived from the Greek word for womb. Women, at the mercy of their reproductive cycle, were seen as fickle, childish, capricious and bad-tempered, making it easy for Antis to argue that women were unlikely to make rational judgements about politics. In a House of Commons debate on women's suffrage in 1871, one MP commented that because reason predominated in the man and emotion in the woman it was foolish to grant votes for women: it would mean a House of Commons dominated by sentiment at the expense of logic. Generally, Antis dwelt on the defects of temperament and intellect of women and argued that, as women saw politics in personal terms, they were absorbed with the trivial and the domestic rather than the more important high politics.

Antis also believed that it was God's wish that men should rule and women be governed. Biblical references to Adam and Eve were made: Eve was formed from the spare rib of Adam and so was subject to his rule. It was therefore argued that the sexes occupied two separate spheres: politics was part of the public sphere of men. It was the responsibility of the male head of household to defend his family, to go out to work and to run the political system. Mrs Humphrey Ward, a famous novelist of the day and the first President of the Anti-Suffrage League, maintained in 1889 that certain government departments should be the exclusive preserve of men:

1   To men belong the struggle of debate and legislation in Parliament; the hard and exhausting labour implied in the administration of the national resources and powers; the conduct of England's relations towards the external world; the working of the army and navy; all the
5   heavy, laborious, fundamental industries of the State, such as those of mines, metals, and railways; the lead and supervision of English commerce, the management of our vast English finance, the service of that merchant fleet on which our food supply depends. In all these spheres women's direct participation is made impossible either by the
10 disabilities of sex, or by strong formations of custom and habit resting ultimately upon physical difference, against which it is useless to

> contend ... Therefore it is not just to give to women direct power of deciding questions of Parliamentary policy, of war, of foreign or colonial affairs, of commerce and finance equal to that possessed by men.[6]

In contrast, the women's role was firmly located in the private sphere of the home and its locality. Mrs Parker Smith, married to an MP and President of a Scottish Women's Liberal Unionist Association, did not agree with votes for women: she believed that women could never play a full part in public life because of their role as wives and mothers. Family life would be destroyed if women gained the vote, she believed, because they would challenge the authority of the male. And as the family was perceived to be the bedrock of society, then it followed that society would be destroyed.

The Antis often spoke of politics being too dirty a game for women. Polling booths were considered unfit places for women because men were often bribed with drink, making polling a raucous and disorderly event. Certainly, before the introduction of the secret ballot in 1872, elections were often seen as the excuse for a riotous party. Women were considered to be far too delicate to enter into the fray of this particular form of politics. Antis even argued that sensible men sent their wives and families away from home during elections because they feared for their safety. To involve women in the tumult of politics would be unseemly and to solicit their votes distinctly improper in case it defiled their natural modesty. As the Liberal Prime Minister Gladstone stated it would 'trespass upon their delicacy, their purity, their refinement and the elevation of their whole nature'. Not surprisingly it was argued that the courtesies which women received from men would cease if women gained the vote because it would rob them of their feminine charms.

Some Antis certainly viewed the campaign for women's suffrage as the action of a few crazy, dissatisfied spinsters and drew attention to the small numbers of women who belonged to suffrage societies or engaged in suffrage activities. They were firmly convinced that the majority of women did not want the vote and were by nature devoid of any direct interest in the affairs of state. Most women, they understood, wished to remain at home looking after their husband and children and that 'the House of Commons had no right to force upon women a privilege which only a very limited number of their sex asked for'.[7] Consequently, the Antis believed that women's suffrage was not yet ripe for legislative action.

c) Male Influence

Antis argued that it was unnecessary for women to be enfranchised because they were already indirectly represented by the men in their family. In the first part of the nineteenth century Parliament was held to represent communities rather than individuals, so a landowner was to represent the village community, a mine owner the mining community - and a husband the interests of his wife and children. In addition, women exerted a subtle and indirect control on national affairs as the wives and mothers of powerful men, through their political hostessing and by bending the ear of the famous. Both Disraeli and Gladstone, for example, kept their wives informed of all Government secrets, whereas Winston Churchill was more receptive to the ideas of the political hostess, Lady Jeune.

Rather inconsistently, fears were also expressed that women were incapable of forming their own opinions and were overly influenced by the men in their lives. Husbands and fathers, in particular, expected their wives and daughters to agree with their political views: opponents suggested that this would have the effect of giving two or more votes to men with close female relatives. In addition, it was feared that religious rivalry, particularly in Ireland, would increase once women were granted the vote. Roman Catholic priests were said to favour female suffrage because of the undue influence they might exercise in the pulpit and the confessional. As a consequence it was feared that the Catholic vote would increase which in turn might create further tensions between Catholic and non-Catholic communities as the former demanded greater equality.

Antis, again inconsistently, believed that the moral and social order would collapse if women were enfranchised because they would not listen to men. On the assumption that electors voted according to their own self-interest, women were expected to vote for issues relevant to their own gender roles. Antis argued that women would vote as women rather than as individuals and would legislate for social reform and against male interests. For example, great concern was expressed that women might vote for temperance reform and ban the sale of alcohol. And as women would predominate in an electorate (when women voted in the 1929 election, which was the first in Britain with universal suffrage, they constituted 52.7 per cent of the electorate) they would conceivably succeed.

d) Women's Influence Outside Parliament

By the beginning of the twentieth century, however, not all Antis considered women to be such inferior beings. A number of Antis, such as Mrs Humphrey Ward, thought it appropriate for women to engage in local politics and argued that women should focus on elevating the tone of public affairs through their religious, educational and charitable work rather than busy themselves with national politics. Indeed local politics was seen as housekeeping on a grander scale and so did not undermine the principles of the separate spheres. The leaflet on page 24, while recognising that women played an important part in local government, maintained that Parliament remained the province of men.

Against Woman Suffrage **by Grace Saxon Mills (early 20th century)**

1 **Because** women already have the municipal vote, and are eligible for membership of most local authorities. These bodies deal with questions of housing, education, care of children, workhouses and so forth, all of which are peculiarly within a woman's sphere.
5 Parliament, however, has to deal mainly with the administration of a vast Empire, the maintenance of the Army and Navy, and with questions of peace and war, which lie outside the legitimate sphere of woman's influence.

Because all government rests ultimately on force, to which women,
10 owing to physical, moral and social reasons, are not capable of contributing.

Because women are not capable of full citizenship, for the simple reason that they are not available for purposes of national and Imperial defence. All government rests ultimately on force, to which
15 women, owing to physical, moral and social reasons, are not capable of contributing.

Because there is little doubt that the vast majority of women have no desire for the vote.

Because the acquirement of the Parliamentary vote would logically
20 involve admission to Parliament itself, and to all Government offices. It is scarcely possible to imagine a woman being Minister for War, and yet the principles of the Suffragettes involve that and many similar absurdities.

Because the United Kingdom is not an isolated state, but the
25 administrative and governing centre of a system of colonies and also of dependencies. The effect of introducing a large female element into the Imperial electorate would undoubtedly be to weaken the centre of power in the eyes of these dependent millions.

30 **Because** past legislation in Parliament shows that the interests of women are perfectly safe in the hands of men.

Because Woman Suffrage is based on the idea of the equality of the sexes, and tends to establish those competitive relations which will destroy chivalrous consideration.

35 **Because** women have at present a vast indirect influence through their menfolk on the politics of this country.

Because the physical nature of women unfits them for direct competition with men.

3 Conclusion

Both sides advanced powerful arguments, but it is fair to say that, at first, the Antis seemed to be winning the debate as the campaign for votes for women was treated as a joke by large numbers of people in Britain. Early suffragists had to be particularly careful in their speeches and their leaflets to advance a rational defence whereas all the Antis had to do was laugh at them to gain support. By 1914, however, many of the ideas of the Antis appeared ludicrously old-fashioned and it was evident that the argument for votes for women had, more or less, been won. Both sides, however, considered that their own particular assertions were correct and, therefore, the debate could not be decided intellectually. Instead, political pressure would play a decisive role in the case for and against women's suffrage.

Suffragists and suffragettes developed numerous justifications for women's franchise but what is remarkable is the consistency of those arguments over time. Indeed there were no specifically 'suffragist' and 'suffragette' justifications. Both groups claimed the right for women to vote on the same terms as men in Parliamentary elections although, as the nineteenth century progressed, the meaning of this demand changed. The first women's suffrage bill in 1870 was decidedly elitist, as only a very few rich women would have been enfranchised, whereas by 1914, as the property qualification for men was lowered, more and more women would be eligible to vote. What did change was the confidence with which the case was argued; whereas early suffragists very tentatively argued their point, the Edwardian suffragettes, more secure in the justice of their cause, produced the most startling propaganda in support. Similarly, both the suffragists and the suffragettes saw the vote as a symbol of citizenship in a democratic country and argued for women to be represented. It used to be assumed that whereas the suffragists wanted the vote as a means to an end, the suffragettes wanted the vote as an end in itself, but this interpretation has recently been revised. The literature produced by both groups suggests that they wanted the vote to end the economic, social and moral exploitation of women. However, there were some differences in practice. For example, Victorian suffragists were more reluctant to associate sexual morality with the vote as it was felt to be harmful to the suffrage cause. In contrast, the Edwardians had few such qualms, Christabel Pankhurst, for instance, held no such fears and promoted the two simultaneously.

The arguments of the Antis, on the other hand, grew more rational over time. When women's suffrage was first debated it was considered so ridiculous that the Antis did not bother to marshal any argument against it at all. This had changed by the end of the nineteenth century as a better organised opposition emerged. Nonetheless, just as with those who campaigned for women's suffrage, there were different bodies of opinion: Mrs Humphrey Ward, for example, maintained that women were different but not unequal to men whereas others still continued to stress women's innate inferiority.

Although the arguments used by those who supported and those who opposed women's suffrage largely differed, there were some surprising similarities. Firstly, most of those involved in the suffrage debate seemed to believe that votes for women was the means to an end. The suffragists, suffragettes and the Antis all held that the vote would bring about a social revolution, but whereas the former welcomed such change it struck fear into the opposition. Suffragists and suffragettes looked forward to the day when women would be able to end the perceived exploitation of their sex by instituting legal changes and increasing educational and employment opportunities. For them, the vote would herald a new dawn of equality. In contrast, the Antis feared the reforming zeal of enfranchised women because it would undermine the authority of the male. One late nineteenth-century MP maintained that a Parliament elected by women would 'have more class cries, permissive legislation, domestic perplexities, and sentimental grievances' and give greater importance to questions of a social nature, at the expense of constitutional and international issues.

Secondly, the suffragists, the suffragettes and their opponents recognised women's contribution to local government. Those who supported women's suffrage used this to convince people of women's ability to engage in national politics, whereas the Antis used the same argument to demonstrate that women had already fulfiled their political potential. In fact, some Antis considered local government to be women's proper sphere because it concerned education, health and housing. Thirdly, both the Suffragists and the Antis were conscious of Britain's role as an imperial power and used this to argue either for or against votes for women. At times both used white supremacist arguments: the suffragists believing that white women should gain the vote before black men; the Antis believing that black men would not accept the authority of women whatever their colour. Such similarities are perhaps not surprising, as after all, the suffragists, the suffragettes and their opposition occupied the same cultural world and historical period. And of course one has to have common areas of agreement in order to disagree!

References

1 Christabel Pankhurst, 'The Great Scourge and How to Fight It' in
   S. Jeffreys, *The Sexuality Debates* (Routledge and Kegan Paul, 1987), p. 318.
2 Antoinette Burton, 'The White Woman's Burden, British Feminists and
   the Indian woman, 1865-1915', *Women's Studies International Forum*, 1990,
   p. 295.
3 Ibid, p.304.
4 Asquith, in Brian Harrison, *Separate Spheres* (Croom Helm, 1978), p. 33.
5 Mrs Frederick Harrison, 1909 in Harrison, *Separate Spheres*, p. 80.
6 From Jane Lewis, *Before the Vote was Won* (Routledge and Kegan Paul,
   1987), p. 409.
7 Ibid, p. 65.

Source-based questions on 'Women's Suffrage: the Debate'

1 Reasons why women wanted the vote

Read the extracts from the suffragists and the Antis quoted on page 19 and page 24 and answer the following questions.

a) Explain what is meant by 'The legislature in the past has not made laws which are equal between men and women' (line 12). (4 marks)

b) How might an opponent of women's suffrage argue against this statement? (4 marks)

c) What similarities and differences are there between the ideas in these two extracts? Refer to particular passages. (8 marks)

d) Would you judge these extracts to be representative of the arguments put forward by the suffragists and their opponents? Explain your answer. (9 marks)

Hints and Advice

Students are often asked to analyse sources in examinations. There are two types of questions which may be asked. The first may ask you to comment on the source in general, whereas the second may ask particular questions of the source. Whatever the type of question you must make sure that you understand the piece of evidence, so read it through carefully to make sure you understand it. However, the source does not stand alone, so it is equally important that you place it within a historical context. Use your knowledge of the period as a whole to help you interpret the source and remember that it is quality not quantity that gets the best mark.

The first question (a) asks you to be quite specific about the meaning of language, whereas the second (b) demands a response. Use both of these questions to demonstrate your knowledge of the period. For instance, in (a) suffragists were concerned that Parliament had in the past enacted laws such as the Divorce Reform Act of 1857 which disadvantaged women. In contrast, their opponents would point to various reforms such as the Married Women's

Property Acts of 1870 and 1882 which benefited women. On the other hand, some Antis might agree with the statement, without being at all critical of it, because women and men weren't considered equal!

For (c) it is best to take each point separately. First of all look at the similarities. For this you need to make both very precise and very general comments. For example, both sides used a similar format, both recognised that the municipal franchise precipitated reform, and both agreed that women's place was in the home. The tone of each source is also quite moderate and seems to appeal to reason rather than emotion. Nevertheless, there are some important differences. For example, the suffragists saw the municipal vote as another step towards the Parliamentary vote whereas their opponents viewed it as the last rung in the ladder of progress. What other differences are there?

For (d) you need a balanced approach for this is a 'yes and no' type of question: on the one hand it is representative but on the other hand it is not. When you are asked to comment on a source it is helpful to bear the following questions in mind: *who* created the source?, *when* was it written?, *what* does it say?, *why* was it created? and *where* was it created? You might like to use these 'five Ws' when you answer this question and others like them. To some extent these arguments were representative of these particular groups (who) at this moment in time (when), but there was quite a lot missed out (what). The suffragist source, for example, does not raise the issue of sexual morality whereas the Antis source, for example, does not raise the issue of inherent female mental instability. Can you think why these might have been omitted? Don't forget that both of these sources were created (why) for publicity purposes.

Summary Diagram

Votes for Women: The Debate

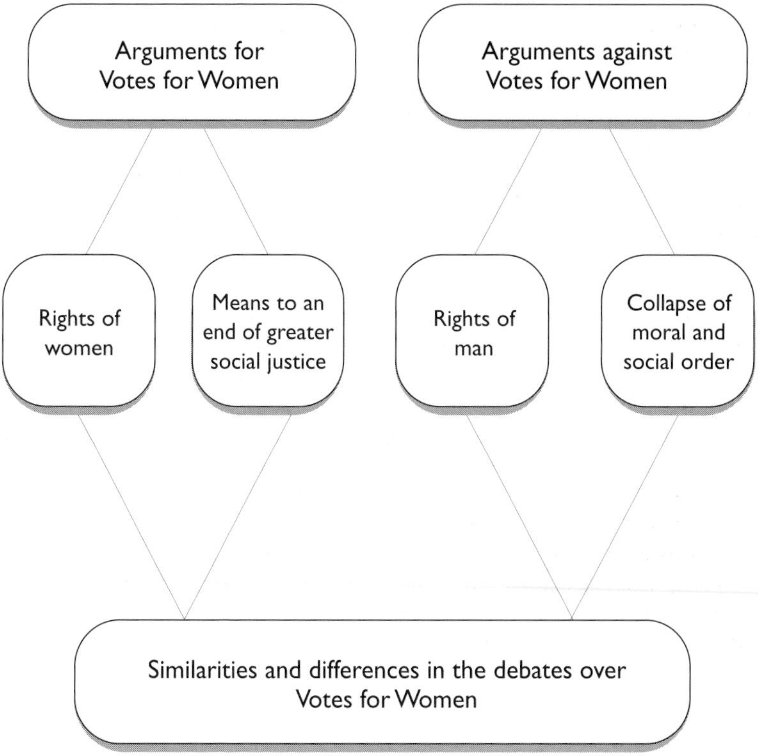

3 Suffragists and Suffragettes

1 The Origins of Women's Suffrage

a) Introduction

In 1860, when this book begins, there were no women's suffrage societies campaigning for votes for women whatsoever, but by 1914 there were approximately 56 groups with a combined membership of 300,000. It is difficult to trace the origins of the women's suffrage movement which operated in late Victorian and Edwardian Britain since, like most political crusades, it had somewhat confused and erratic beginnings. The suffrage movement began slowly with several people in different towns thinking and agitating around similar issues, in this case the vote. Some historians date the movement from 1832, when Mary Smith presented the first women's suffrage petition to Parliament. The letters and the leaflets distributed in support of women's suffrage by Anne Knight in 1847, and the Sheffield Female Political Association formed in 1851, are also considered key moments of suffrage history. Others date the origins of the suffrage movement much later and suggest that it really took off in 1867, when John Stuart Mill moved an amendment to the Second Reform Bill asking that the word 'man' be replaced by 'person'. Nevertheless, the publication of certain texts - Mary Wollstonecraft's *A Vindication of the Rights of Women* in 1792; William Thompson's wordily titled *Appeal of One Half the Human Race, Women, Against the Pretensions of the Other Half, Men, to Retain Them in Political, and Thence in Civil and Domestic Slavery* in 1825; and Harriet Taylor and J. S. Mill's *The Subjection of Women* in 1869 - are seen to be important because they established the intellectual argument for votes for women.

Historians nevertheless agree that London and Manchester were the major suffragist centres and that the year 1866 was a significant landmark in suffragist history. In that year some of the most notable feminist campaigners of the nineteenth century - Barbara Bodichon, Emily Davies, Jessie Boucherett, Elizabeth Garrett and Helen Taylor - drafted a petition to Parliament demanding the enfranchisement of all householders regardless of sex. Emily Davies and Elizabeth Garrett carried the petition, signed by almost 1,500 women, to the House of Commons where two of the handful of sympathetic MPs, J. S. Mill and Henry Fawcett, presented it. In 1866 too, the Manchester National Society for Women's Suffrage was formed followed shortly after by similar organisations in Birmingham, Bristol, Edinburgh and Ireland. Each of these groups was independent but in 1868 they amalgamated to become the National Society for Women's Suffrage. This, according to most historians, was the moment when organised national action began.

b) Uneasy Alliances

This unity was not to last as the early women's suffrage movement was characterised by internal divisions. Like other political associations with just one goal, and often without any real power, the suffragists and later the suffragettes, differed over the best way to achieve their objective. Consequently, those campaigning for votes for women have had a rather complex and chequered history which the summary on page 45 helps to explain.

At the outset, the London group witnessed a number of disagreements over strategy between two of the most powerful advocates of women's suffrage: Helen Taylor and Barbara Bodichon. These internal wranglings led to many suffragists disassociating themselves from the London group, thus weakening the emerging women's movement. It is not surprising therefore that the first London society was seen to be ineffective.

Another split occurred between London and the rest of the country in response to the Ladies National Association's (LNA) campaigns against the Contagious Diseases Acts (CDAs) (see page 5). On the one hand members of the provincial suffrage societies considered the LNA and the women's suffrage movement to be part of the same struggle against female oppression. In their opinion, the CDAs were part of a male conspiracy by a male House of Parliament and would not have been passed if women had voting power. On the other hand, the London National Society for Women's Suffrage wished to keep women's suffrage distinct from other political protest groups, not because they were antagonistic to the LNA, but because they feared it might create unnecessary enemies for the suffrage cause. As a consequence, the NSWS split into two, and not until 1877 did the two organisations reunite to form the Central Committee of the National Society.

Finally, at the end of 1888 yet another split occurred, precipitated by two major disagreements over political strategy. Firstly a number of - mostly younger and radical - suffragists wanted to affiliate to the women's section of the Liberal Association because the Liberal Party was perceived to be sympathetic to votes for women. Others - mostly the older members - disagreed because they wanted to keep the suffrage organisation independent of party politics. Secondly, younger members wanted to link suffrage with other female reforms (in particular the campaign for greater property rights), while the older members preferred to keep suffrage distinct. Once again the suffrage movement split into two, rather confusingly named, groups: the National Central Society for Women's Suffrage and the Central Committee of the National Society for Women's Suffrage. This particular schism - which lasted until 1897 - coincided with a time of comparative inaction.

As well as all these faction-fighting groups, the Women's Franchise

League (formed in 1889) and the Women's Emancipation Union (formed in 1892) added another two voices to the women's suffrage contest. Both of these groups were founded because of a dissatisfaction with the 'spinsterish' policies of the other societies. They established links with international suffrage groups, supported the newly emerging labour movement and campaigned for radical measures such as equal pay for equal work. Nevertheless all the numerous splits and divisions which occurred in the suffrage movement of the nineteenth century paved the way for the new organisational directions of the twentieth.

2 The NUWSS and its Offshoots: 1897-1914

There was a high level of social homogeneity (that is uniformity) within the suffrage movement since most leaders of the NUWSS shared a family and friendship circle and held similar political convictions and religious beliefs. Although the NUWSS claimed to be non-party political, many suffragists had links with the Liberal Party or were sympathetic to Liberal aims and had access to the Liberal political elite. Many were also joint members of the Women's Liberal Federation and the NUWSS and were often the wives, mothers or daughters of prominent Liberal politicians. For example, Helen Taylor, the daughter of Harriet Taylor, enjoyed an unusually close relationship with her step-father, the highly respected Liberal philosopher John Stuart Mill, who championed the cause of women's suffrage in Parliament. Similarly, Catherine Osler, leader of the Birmingham NUWSS and President of the Women's Auxiliary of the Liberal Association, was sister in law to the prominent Liberal Joseph Chamberlain.

Politics was firmly linked to religion. A number of suffragists came from Nonconformist radical backgrounds in which political and social reform was on the agenda: apparently 20 per cent of the executive of the NUWSS were Quakers.

It is not surprising that, given their political and religious background, many suffragist leaders belonged to families who were committed to social reform in a wider context. Millicent Fawcett, for example, was the daughter of a merchant who was sympathetic to feminism, the younger sister of the first English woman doctor, the widow of a former Liberal Cabinet Minister, and a close friend of John Stuart Mill. Brian Harrison argues that 'her feminism reflected all the fierce middle class commitment to an opportunity society, all the strenuous Liberal faith in liberty and progress, that had motivated the nineteenth century's anti-slavery and free-trade crusades'.[1] Millicent Fawcett was not exceptional in this respect. Years earlier, the Quaker suffragist Anne Knight was actively involved in the abolitionist movement, supported free trade, the Chartists and sympathised with European republicanism.[2] Indeed, there were 'suffrage families' such as Priscilla Bright MacLaren's: her brother, Jacob Bright, had defended women's suffrage in Parliament and her sons and daughters-in-law were all women's suffrage activists.

Not surprisingly, many suffragists were also involved in other women's rights issues. Both Barbara Bodichon and Emmeline Wolstoneholme Elmy had led campaigns to reform the Married Women's Property Acts (see page 4). Experience such as this provided a bridge between women's traditional role in the private sphere of the home and their future one in the public sphere of political struggle. And of course the kinship, friendship, religious and political circle to which they belonged provided women with the emotional and moral support needed to lead an unconventional campaign.

In their thought-provoking book, Liddington and Norris broke the myth that the suffrage movement was completely dominated by the middle class. Certainly, the membership of the NUWSS was socially mixed in the north of England. In some areas like Oldham it was predominantly middle class, whereas a few miles away in Clitheroe the membership was exclusively working class. One of the associations affiliated to the NUWSS, the North of England Society for Women's Suffrage, was committed to broadening the class composition of the suffrage movement and so put a great deal of effort into recruiting working-class women.

Nevertheless, there were certain tensions between the older middle-class members of the NUWSS and the newer working-class recruits of the North of England Society. In 1903 the Lancashire and Cheshire Women Textile and Other Workers Representation Committee (LCWT) was founded specifically for working-class women. Although it was set up by the university educated Esther Roper and the aristocratic Eva Gore-Booth, they encouraged working-class women to participate at a senior level: several textile workers and trade union activists took a leading role in the North of England Society. Not surprisingly, the LCWT worked closely with the Women's Co-operative Guild and the Manchester and Salford Women's Trade Union Council, of which Eva Gore Booth was Co-Secretary. Although the LCWT had broken away from the NUWSS, the two groups - unlike those of the nineteenth century - were not antagonistic towards each other. On the contrary, the LCWT received a lot of financial help from the NUWSS with the result that it was able to establish support for women's suffrage in the textile towns of the north of England.

By the end of the nineteenth century the women's suffrage movement appeared to be united and strong, with NUWSS branches all over Britain (see the map on page 34). In 1910 the membership had grown to 21,571. Just before the outbreak of war there were approximately 400 societies in England, Scotland and Wales. However, the suffragists were to face new challenges in the early twentieth century

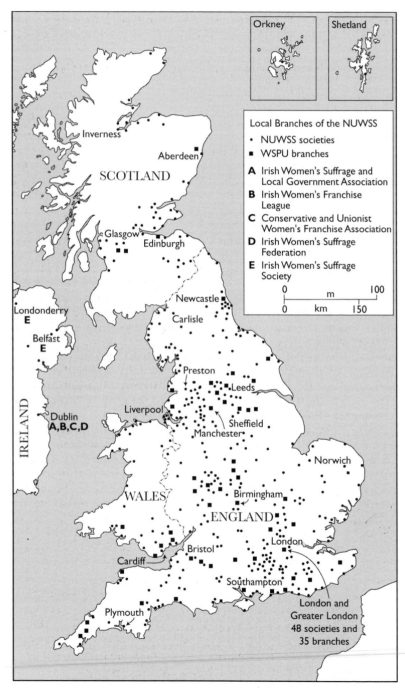

Orkney

Shetland

Inverness

Aberdeen

SCOTLAND

Local Branches of the NUWSS

- • NUWSS societies
- ■ WSPU branches

A Irish Women's Suffrage and Local Government Association
B Irish Women's Franchise League
C Conservative and Unionist Women's Franchise Association
D Irish Women's Suffrage Federation
E Irish Women's Suffrage Society

Glasgow
Edinburgh

```
0           m          100
0          km         150
```

Londonderry
E

Newcastle

Carlisle

Belfast
E

Preston

Leeds

Liverpool

Sheffield

IRELAND

Dublin
A,B,C,D

Manchester

Norwich

WALES

Birmingham

ENGLAND

Bristol

London

Cardiff

Southampton

London and Greater London 48 societies and 35 branches

Plymouth

Adapted from Di Atkinson's Votes for Women, *1988*

when a new organisation, the Women's Social and Political Union (WSPU) erupted onto the political scene.

3 The WSPU and its Offshoots: 1903-1914

a) Structure of the Organisation

In 1903 Emmeline Pankhurst, who had been active in previous suffrage campaigns, founded the Women's Social and Political Union (WSPU) at her house in Manchester. The decision to form a new association was prompted by dissatisfaction with both the Labour Party (which was seen to be too lukewarm in its support of women's suffrage), and the NUWSS (which was seen to be too cautious). In January 1906 the *Daily Mail* coined the word - 'suffragette' - for the WSPU members: the name stuck. From this time onwards, the suffrage movement was to be dominated by two main groups: the suffragists of the NUWSS and the suffragettes of the WSPU.

It is widely accepted that the WSPU was an autocratic, man-hating, organisation which was considerably less democratic than its rival. From 1906, policies were decided by an unelected Central Committee with Sylvia Pankhurst as secretary, Emmeline Pethick Lawrence as Treasurer and Annie Kenney as paid organiser. This Central Committee was assisted by a sub-committee which consisted of family and friends such as Mary Clarke (Emmeline Pankhurst's sister). Members did not participate in decision making but were informed of new policies and strategies during the 'At Homes' sessions, which were held each Monday afternoon at the headquarters in Lincoln's Inn Field, London. The leadership controlled their own publications, appointments to paid positions and of course the finances of the organisation, making it difficult for members to oppose them.

Historians have criticised this structure. Ray Strachey, for instance, suggests that the WSPU 'entrusted all their decisions to their leaders ... These people alone decided what was to be done; the others obeyed, and enjoyed the surrender of their judgement, and the sensation of marching as an army under discipline.'[3] Similarly, George Dangerfield views the WSPU as a dictatorial organisation under the dual tyranny of Emmeline Pankhurst and her daughter Christabel. He believes that Christabel Pankhurst's

1 inexplicable combination of feminine caprice and masculine steel, became, as the months went on, the secret of the WSPU ... With the departure of the Pethick Lawrences Miss Christabel and her mother attained the long desired peak of despotic authority ... the seductive
5 personality of Christabel, in London the indefatigable brain of Mrs Pankhurst dictated every move ... above everything, the forms of Emmeline and Christabel Pankhurst scour the furious scene like a pair of risen but infernal queens.[4]

David Mitchell not only entitles the last chapter of his book *Queen Christabel*, 'Bitch Power', as an unflattering description of the suffragettes and their successors, but compares the WSPU with the Baader-Meinhof German terrorist gang.[5] Socialist feminist historians, although using different terminology, subscribe to this interpretation: Liddington and Norris believe that the leadership of the WSPU exercised draconian control over its membership. One suffragette at the time commented that although Emmeline Pankhurst 'wishes women to have votes she will not allow them to have opinions'.[6]

Critics disapproved of the organisational structure of the WSPU for a number of reasons: it was considered hypocritical of the WSPU to condemn the Liberal Government for its reluctance to widen the suffrage while failing to practise democracy itself; it was believed that the vote should be sought through a democratic organisation which mirrored a future body politic rather than one which clearly did not; and it was thought that unquestioning obedience to a female oligarchy was inadequate preparation for the future female voter, who needed to evaluate the arguments of each political party.

However, although the WSPU was undoubtedly dictatorial in style and had no formal constitution, there are a number of points to take into consideration before it is condemned out of hand. Firstly, critics of the WSPU's structure are largely those in sympathy with the NUWSS and who thus take sides in the suffrage struggle. Secondly, the WSPU was not always undemocratic. Initially it favoured an informal approach to politics - there was no official membership list and any woman who wished to attend a meeting was welcome. In the beginning neither Christabel nor Emmeline Pankhurst took an officer role because they feared their new organisation might be dubbed the Pankhurst family party. As time went on, it is true, the WSPU did become more formalised and less democratic. Nevertheless, nobody was forced to belong to the organisation and members could always leave if they disagreed with the policies. And Harrison remarks ironically that 'the seven splits and numerous individual secessions between 1903 and 1914 show that dissidents were indeed free to depart'.[7] Thirdly, as both Emmeline and Christabel Pankhurst argued, a democratic organisation was probably inappropriate for their style of politics. Indeed the WSPU became less democratic as its activities became more illegal. And as the WSPU increasingly operated within a hostile political climate, so planning and action assumed greater importance than constitutional democracy. Fourthly, the WSPU did educate its membership, encouraged their self-confidence and helped to develop political awareness. Many a suffragette spoke of the way in which they were taught the skills of public speaking and debate. Finally, although the London-based WSPU was undoubtedly undemocratic, this may not have been the case for the provincial branches and their regional offices. In 1909 there were at least 11 regional offices, in the West of England (with offices in Bristol and Torquay), Lancashire (with offices in Manchester, Preston and Rochdale), Birmingham, Leeds, Newcastle, Glasgow, Edinburgh and Aberdeen. And as the map on page 34 shows, the WSPU had numerous branches elsewhere. For the most part, these branches and offices enjoyed considerable autonomy, as the following extract from an Annual Report suggests:

1 In all parts of London and in many provincial centres, there exist local
   Unions which, while working in close and harmonious relation with
   the National headquarters, are independent in the sense that they
   elect their own committee, and administer their own funds ... and
5 arrange their own schemes of organisation and propaganda.[8]

The East London Federation of Suffragettes (ELFS), a working-class branch of the WSPU organised by another daughter of Emmeline Pankhurst, Sylvia, was certainly run on democratic lines with officers and delegates voted in.[9] The points outlined above may not overthrow the hostile criticism made of the WSPU but they certainly modify it by explaining the context in which the suffragettes worked.

Concern is also expressed by historians that the suffragettes were anti-male and in favour of almost worshipping women. It is certainly true that the WSPU would not allow men to join the organisation and continually affirmed women's independence from the opposite sex. Yet the WSPU initially welcomed male support. In particular, it appreciated the advice of Frederick Pethick Lawrence who helped edit *Votes for Women* and whose business acumen helped lift the economic fortunes of the WSPU from a small provincial society to a great business enterprise. Nonetheless, by 1913 the WSPU was unwilling to co-operate with men or with organisations, like the NUWSS, which had male associates. Radical feminist historians are not so critical of this shift for they view the WSPU as the first autonomous women's organisation and therefore the precursor of the women's liberation movement of the late 1960s.

b) Suffragette Membership

One of the major criticisms levelled against the WSPU relates to its membership, which is compared unfavourably with that of the NUWSS. Historians have argued that the WSPU was an elitist organisation committed to an elitist franchise. Certainly, the WSPU was associated with middle-class and aristocratic spinsters who wanted a limited franchise based on property qualifications rather than universal suffrage. However, this criticism needs reassessment. The founder of the WSPU, Emmeline Pankhurst, came from a similar social background to the members of the NUWSS. She, like Millicent Fawcett, sprang from a long line of male political activists. She was the granddaughter of a man who had demonstrated at Peterloo, daughter of a radical cotton manufacturer, and wife of a left-wing lawyer,

Richard Pankhurst. What is more, the WSPU at first recruited greater numbers of working-class women than the NUWSS, for the roots of the WSPU lay in the Labour politics of the north of England rather than the Liberal salons of the south. It was set up specifically for working-class women and between 1903 and 1906 did valuable propaganda work in the textile towns. Even when the WSPU's headquarters moved to London it targeted working-class women. When Annie Kenney, a cotton worker recruited at a WSPU meeting in Oldham, and Sylvia Pankhurst were sent to London to organise the campaign in the capital most of their energies were spent in working-class districts. Moreover, the first London branch of the WSPU was formed at Canning Town in the East End.

Yet, when Christabel Pankhurst arrived in London working-class women receded into the background of the WSPU to be replaced by women of an entirely different social class. The most famous example was the aristocratic and politically Conservative Constance Lytton, whose father had been one of the Viceroys of India and whose mother had been lady-in-waiting to Queen Victoria. Historians have condemned the WSPU for recruiting upper-class women. Andrew Rosen, for example, regrets the decline of working-class membership, particularly when the WSPU 'ceased to envisage votes for women as a measure desirable primarily because it would benefit working class women'.[10] Liddington and Norris, too, criticise the WSPU because it had little sustained contact with working-class women.

In many ways this analysis only really applies to the central London section, for the WSPU's strength lay with its local branches as much as its headquarters. Until 1908 the WSPU was active in Woolwich, Lewisham and Greenwich, working with the local Labour Party to recruit working-class women. Sylvia Pankhurst's ELFS remained a working-class organisation and 'regarded itself as part of the labour movement, for it saw the achievement of equality and emancipation as inseparable from a socialist organisation of society'.[11] In Scotland too the links with working-class women and socialism remained strong. Furthermore, whatever its class composition, the WSPU supported working-class women's issues. For instance, when working-class women such as pit-brow workers, chain makers and barmaids, had their livelihoods threatened they each received support from the WSPU.

It could also be argued that the recruitment of middle and upper-class women to the WSPU may not have been a weakness at all because this broadening of its class composition made it less exclusive. Moreover, in bringing women from different classes together, the WSPU helped weaken the class divisions which characterised Edwardian Britain. Certainly the WSPU saw the unity of women as more important than the division of class and suggested that the subordination of women to men was as at least as significant as class oppression. This prompted the radical feminist historian Elizabeth

Sarah to argue that 'what these early feminists were doing was laying claims to sexual equality by challenging the power of men'.[12] By 1914 Christabel Pankhurst undoubtedly treated all men as enemies, complained that socialist men - despite their commitment to equality - were little better than the Conservatives and Liberals in their failure to support votes for women and even considered her godfather Frederick Pethick Lawrence (who had devoted his life to the cause) to be an embarrassment purely because he was a man.

c) Divisions within the WSPU

It is sometimes argued that the splits in the WSPU arose primarily because the Pankhursts were ruthless in getting rid of those who criticised their personal control. Between 1903 and 1914 there were seven splits in the WSPU. The three most important splits occurred in 1907, 1912 and 1914 respectively. The first split involved Teresa Billington-Greig, Charlotte Despard and others; the second the Pethick Lawrences; and the third, Sylvia Pankhurst.

During 1907 differences came to a head between Charlotte Despard, Teresa Billington-Greig and Emmeline Pankhurst. The first two expressed concern that the WSPU was turning its back on the working class and cultivating upper-class and wealthy women. More importantly, Teresa Billington-Greig wanted greater organisational democracy and further autonomy for the branches. In 1906 she drafted a democratic constitution which would have given the WSPU Annual Conferences with elected leaders and members who could vote. In effect, the proposed constitution, which had been accepted by much of the membership, placed power in the hands of the branch delegates at the expense of the leadership. Unfortunately for Billington-Greig, Emmeline and Christabel Pankhurst disagreed with it, and in a well orchestrated coup d'état denounced the leaders as conspirators, tore up the proposed constitution and formed a new committee composed of those sympathetic to the Pankhurst doctrine.

The following extract written by Billington-Greig soon after the split certainly expresses a deep hostility towards the Pankhursts, but it also confirms some historians' views that the Pankhurst leadership dealt with criticism by ignoring it.

1   When the Conference day came it was attended by delegates and
     individual members indiscriminately who assembled ready for
     discussion on constructive lines. But instead of discussion, there was
     an announcement of dictatorship put forward with all the eloquence,
5   skill and feeling of which Mrs Pankhurst was capable. The draft
     Constitution was dramatically torn up and thrown to the ground. The
     assembled members were informed that they were in the ranks in an
     army of which she was the permanent Commander-in-Chief.

In response to the rejection of the Constitution, Teresa Billington-

Greig and Charlotte Despard, along with a fifth of the WSPU membership, left to found the Women's Freedom League (WFL). 'If we are fighting against the subjection of woman to man, we cannot honestly submit to the subjection of woman to woman,' said Teresa Billington-Greig.[13]

However, the WFL failed to establish any distinctive image as in many ways it was a hybrid of the WSPU and the NUWSS. On the one hand it was a militant society, engaging in illegal actions, but on the other hand it was democratic and thus it fell between the law-breaking suffragettes and the law-abiding suffragists. Furthermore, although the WFL was supposedly non-party it remained loyal to its Labour origins, worked closely with local Labour groups and campaigned for Labour candidates at elections. Interestingly, the WFL was often beset by internal divisions, making even the rebellious Billington-Greig at times envy the WSPU's alleged autocratic style.

If the Pankhursts were criticised, friendship ties were swiftly broken. Emmeline and Frederick Pethick Lawrence, who were Christabel's close friends were expelled from the WSPU in October 1912. The Pethick Lawrences had not only questioned the escalation of violence but Fred, as the only man ever to take a large part in the running of the WSPU, was seen increasingly as a social embarrassment in an all-female organisation. When Christabel Pankhurst announced that she 'disapproved of men's intimate concern' in the movement it augured badly for Fred's future role within the WSPU. In a remarkable token of generosity, the Pethick Lawrences left the WSPU without acrimony, continued to publish *Votes for Women* and helped found the United Suffragists in early 1914, re-establishing links with the radical section of the Labour movement.

Family ties, too, were broken in the event of disagreement. In January 1914 Sylvia Pankhurst was summoned to Paris by her sister Christabel - who was in voluntary exile there (see page 73) - to be informed that she must either 'toe the line' or sever all links with the WSPU. Christabel informed her that the WSPU must have only one policy, one programme, and one command: those who wished to give an independent lead, or carry out programmes which differed from those laid down by the WSPU must create an independent organisation of their own. Moreover, Christabel Pankhurst disliked her sister's emphasis on class politics. In concentrating her energies in the East End of London, in conducting the campaign for votes for women along class lines and in forming a 'People's Army' to fight against class oppression, Sylvia Pankhurst was thought to discredit the WSPU. And because both sides refused to compromise the ELFS ceased to be a branch of the WSPU and became a separate organisation. This split may have permitted Sylvia Pankhurst the freedom to pursue her own politics but, cut off from the funds of the WSPU, the ELFS did not develop into a significant suffrage organisation. Nonetheless, Sylvia founded her own paper, the *Woman's Dreadnought*, and continued to concentrate on working-class women's suffrage.

Unlike the NUWSS, the WSPU did not divulge its membership, and so figures and composition are difficult to calculate, but there is no doubt that its membership grew rapidly. The 'At Home' attendances in London rose to about 1,000 each week and by 1910 its income was £33, 027. This enabled the WSPU to employ 98 women office workers in London and 26 officers in charge of regional districts. The circulation of *Votes for Women* also increased to between 30,000 and 40,000. However, the wealth of the WSPU declined in 1913. What is more, the WSPU was less successful at a regional level: 34 of its 88 branches were in London.

4 Conclusion

By the outbreak of the First World War it seemed as if the suffrage movement was divided into two major camps: the suffragists and the suffragettes. However, such an analysis is misleading. Certainly, at leadership level there were distinct differences between the two groups but this was not the case among the general membership. Many suffrage supporters joined both a militant and a constitutionalist society, paid two membership fees, attended two sets of meetings and campaigned for both groups. Such women may not have seen the suffrage movement as made up of antagonistic groups vying for members but as one movement with a common aim. Nonetheless, the two organisations were distinct. Undoubtedly, the NUWSS was the more democratic of the two, but we need to consider the importance of this in the heady atmosphere of Edwardian politics. Democracy is time-consuming: leadership has to be elected; votes have to be canvassed; and policies have to be discussed. It could be argued that the emphasis by the NUWSS on internal politics hindered direct action. In stark contrast, the WSPU spent little time discussing policy: in the immortal words of Emmeline Pankhurst, 'Deeds not Words' were paramount. Yet, of course, a group which campaigns for democracy but which does not practise it can be accused of a certain duplicity.

Although these two groups have dominated the historiography of the suffrage movement there were many other societies which have either yet to be researched or are under-researched. Professional women founded their own suffrage societies: the Artists' Franchise League, the Actresses' Franchise League, the London Graduates' League and the Scottish Universities Women's Suffrage Union were amongst them. Similarly different religious denominations set up suffrage groups: the Catholic Women's Suffrage Society, the Church League for Women's Suffrage, the Free Church League, the Friends' League and the Jewish League represented women from a variety of religious backgrounds. Women even set up suffrage organisations which reflected their political affiliations, such as the Conservative and Unionist Women's Franchise Association. From this list it seems as if most women were able to join a suffrage group which represented their profession, religion or political affiliation. However, the membership of these groups may have over-lapped with the two national bodies.

More importantly, despite the recent publication of a few excellent books (see page 120), there is still too little information about the suffrage movement in Ireland, Scotland and Wales. It is known that the NUWSS and the WSPU had active branches all over Scotland and Wales, whereas there were several Irish independent organisations: one of the most influential was the Irish Women's Franchise League (IWFL) founded in 1908. The lack of research on these groups raises wider historical questions about the Anglocentrism (where everything is considered in terms of England) of historians who have generally ignored the suffrage movement in the rest of the British Isles. It also raises questions about whether or not female unity was able to rise above national identity: the IWFL was formed because Irish women, like many of their male compatriots, had no desire to be led by Englishwomen. Unfortunately, the limited amount of published work on the suffrage movement outside England means that it is hard to make any worthwhile judgement.

The formation of so many different suffrage societies and the many divisions which occurred within them raise further questions about female solidarity. The suffrage movement, although a woman's movement, seemed to be little different from other reform groups in that it was characterised by political bickering and internal wrangling. In many ways, despite their negative comments, historians tend to have higher expectations of women than they do of men and are surprised when women - often assumed to be more co-operative and conciliatory - disagree so vehemently. As a consequence, the splits, particularly within the WSPU, are unsympathetically portrayed as female squabbles rather than as serious political differences between intelligent participants.

Socialist historians have undoubtedly corrected the stereotypical image of the female suffragist as a middle-class spinster. They have shown that a significant number of working-class women, particularly in the north of England, participated in the suffrage movement. These findings certainly add a 'politically correct' respectability to the suffrage movement, but one must examine the validity of such a claim as well its relevance. Moreover, there is far too little known about the composition of the suffrage movement at grass roots level, and until historians build up a national picture based upon local research it will be impossible to gauge the extent of working-class support. Certainly at leadership level, the middle classes dominated. Suffrage leaders were usually married to wealthy men or belonged to wealthy families and were undeniably middle or upper middle class. In a political movement which relied upon the unpaid work of women, only those who were economically independent or married to men who were financially secure could afford to engage in political action. For example, the nineteenth century suffragist Lydia Becker was able to devote her life to the suffrage cause because she was not expected to engage in paid work. Similarly, Barbara Bodichon, the daughter of a wealthy radical MP, enjoyed a generously endowed independent income. In the twentieth century, Lady Constance Lytton and Emmeline Pethick Lawrence were wealthy enough not only to support themselves but also to donate large sums of money to the WSPU. Most male political organisations - be they socialist or Conservative - have also been led by the middle class, but historians are not so critical of the class composition of even revolutionary groups. In contrast, historians seem obsessed about the class background of women's groups and one must ask - rather provocatively perhaps - why this is so.

The suffrage movement also had its female opponents. Some women disagreed with votes for women and campaigned against it. In 1889, Mrs Humphrey Ward persuaded 104 prominent women to sign an appeal against female suffrage. Indeed, female antipathy to the vote led to the formation of the Women's National Anti-Suffrage League in 1908. Most women were probably more apathetic than antagonistic towards votes for women. Membership of the suffrage movement may have been large but the majority of women did not belong to any suffrage group.

Despite schisms and irreconcilable differences the women's suffrage movement became a powerful political force within Victorian and Edwardian Britain. By 1914, largely because of its intensive campaigning, it had forced women's suffrage onto the agenda of all the political parties and had made votes for women one of the foremost issues facing the governing Liberal Party.

References
1   Brian Harrison, *Prudent Revolutionaries* (Clarendon Press, 1987), p. 19.
2   Gail Malmgreen, 'Anne Knight and the Radical Subculture', *Quaker History*, 1982, p. 108.
3   Ray Strachey, *The Cause* (Virago Press, 1978), p. 310.
4   George Dangerfield, *The Strange Death of Liberal England* (Perigree Books, 1966), p. 184.
5   Quoted in Elizabeth Sarah 'Christabel Pankhurst: Reclaiming her Power' in Dale Spender, *Feminist Theories* (Woman's Press, 1987) pp. 261-262.
6   Brian Harrison, *Prudent Revolutionaries*, p. 41.
7   Ibid, p. 50.
8   WSPU Annual Report, 1908. p. 7.
9   Barbara Winslow, *Sylvia Pankhurst* (UCL, 1996) p. 46.
10 Andrew Rosen, *Rise Up Women: The Militant Campaign of the WSPU 1903-1914* (Routledge and Kegan Paul, 1974), p. 77.
11 Barbara Winslow, *Sylvia Pankhurst*, p. 41.
12 Elizabeth Sarah, *Feminist Theories*, p. 270.
13 Brian Harrison, *Prudent Revolutionaries*, p. 50.

Source-based questions on 'Suffragists and Suffragettes'

1   The structure of the WSPU

Read the two extracts about the WSPU quoted on pages 35 and 37 and answer the following questions:

a)   What does Dangerfield mean by 'inexplicable combination of feminine caprice and masculine steel' (line 1)? (2 marks)

b)   What is the tone of the comments made by Dangerfield? Illustrate your answer with specific examples. (5 marks)

c)   What is the tone of the WSPU Annual Report and how does it differ from Dangerfield's? Again, illustrate your answer with specific examples. (6 marks)

d)   Would you agree with Dangerfield's comments? Give reasons for your answer. (7 marks)

Summary Diagram
Suffragists and Suffragettes

Was the suffrage movement middle class?

Votes for Women 1860-1914

SUFFRAGISTS

1867 Local societies for Women's Suffrage

 join ...... *join*

1868 **National Society for Women's Suffrage**

 *split* ...... *split*

1872 Central Committee National Society for Women's Suffrage

London National Society for Women's Suffrage

join ...... *join*

1877 Central Committee, National Society for Women's Suffrage

 split ...... *split*

National Central Society for Women's Suffrage

Central Committee, National Society for Women's Suffrage

join ...... *join*

1897 **National Union of Women's Suffrage Societies**

 split

1903 Lancashire and Cheshire Women Textile and Other Workers Representation Committee

SUFFRAGETTES

Women's Social and Political Union

 split

1907 Women's Freedom League split *split*

 split

1912 Pethick Lawrences dismissed

1914 East London Federation of Suffragettes split

Why was there disunity in the suffrage movement?

Why were the Pankhursts autocratic?

Did the lack of unity in the suffrage movement delay the vote?

4 The Suffrage Campaigns

1 Introduction

The story of the few militant suffragettes who were willing to sacrifice their friends, family and - sometimes - their lives to win the vote has gained almost legendary status. However, the historian needs to challenge some of the assumptions that accompany it. Indeed, there are at least two widely held beliefs which need to be questioned. The first, and probably the more important, concerns the difference in political strategies between the suffragists and the suffragettes. In popular belief, the suffragists are assumed to be conventional and law-abiding, whereas the suffragettes have acquired the image of being unconventional and law-breaking. The women's suffrage movement is seen to be split between those (like the National Union of Women's Suffrage Societies, the NUWSS) who favoured moral force and those (like the Women's Social and Political Union, the WSPU) who favoured physical force. At first, it is generally argued, the methods used by all the suffrage groups were peaceful - and legal - but as time went on more violent - and illegal - methods were favoured, particularly by the WSPU. As a consequence the suffragists are deemed to be constitutional, whereas the suffragettes are regarded as militant. Furthermore, in a thought provoking essay Sandra Holton suggests it is important to overcome the 'analytical imprecision' of the term 'militant'.[1] Militancy is an elastic concept which changed its meaning over the fifty or more years in which women campaigned for the vote: suffragists were considered militant in 1860 when they dared to speak at meetings but by 1914 public speaking was seen to be quite acceptable female behaviour.

The second question concerns the relationship between the suffragists and the suffragettes. It is assumed, erroneously, that - because of the differences over political tactics - there was hostility between the various women's suffrage organisations. The NUWSS were said to be antagonistic towards the WSPU because its members used violent methods, whereas the WSPU were said to condemn the NUWSS's lack of imagination. This interpretation too needs to be reassessed, as the NUWSS initially condoned the militancy of the WSPU and held banquets in honour of those who had been imprisoned. The Criterion Restaurant in Piccadilly, London, was even hired to host welcoming parties for women who had just been released from gaol. This support was not to last. The increasingly violent tactics of the WSPU gradually alienated the NUWSS and by 1909 it was voicing public disapproval of the WSPU's tactics. Nevertheless, the divisions between the two groups were not always constant. For example, when the WSPU called a temporary halt to militancy (which, apart from a brief lapse in November 1910, lasted from January 1910 to November

1911) the old spirit of unity reappeared and the suffrage groups organised joint meetings and demonstrations.

2 Legal Methods

Between 1860 and 1914 various methods were used to publicise the issue of votes for women. For most of this time the suffrage movement used peaceful and legitimate measures copied from other reform groups. Early suffragists learned a lot about political tactics from their participation in the Anti-Corn Law campaigns of the early nineteenth century. They discovered how to organise public meetings, demonstrate, write propaganda literature, raise money, lobby MPs and petition Parliament, all traditional middle-class methods of persuasive campaigning. Although the WSPU later adopted a confrontational style they continued to combine more traditional methods with the new.

a) Meetings

All the women's suffrage groups held both semi-private and public meetings to generate publicity and recruit members. Guests were invited to meetings at people's houses to listen to speakers on questions concerning women. Topics included 'The Marriage and Divorce Laws', readings from the works of sympathetic novelists such as Olive Schreiner and, of course, votes for women. Public meetings, initially advertised for women only, were also organised. Lydia Becker and other suffrage workers spoke at mothers' meetings, church groups and political organisations to publicise women's suffrage. The NUWSS raised the question of women's suffrage at trade union conferences and visited most of the major cotton towns to publicise the cause. Public meetings were also organised by the WSPU throughout the country to consolidate support, gain recruits, collect money and sell papers. In 1909, for instance, large meetings were held in the Royal Albert Hall and the Queen's Hall, London; the Colston Hall, Bristol; the Sun Hall, Liverpool; the Albert Hall, Nottingham; the Town Hall, Birmingham; the Synod Hall, Edinburgh; St Andrew's Hall, Glasgow; and the Rotunda, Dublin. Such meetings were carefully orchestrated and planned. In Birmingham, the WSPU divided the city into districts, each with an organiser who had to co-ordinate four small weekly meetings to publicise women's suffrage.The WSPU broke new organisational ground by speaking to audiences in open-air at places such as Trafalgar Square, Blackheath Common and village greens throughout the country. Supporters soon became used to suffragettes speaking wherever women were to be found in large numbers: the local market squares, bus and tram stations, factory gates such as the Cadbury works at Bournville, laundries, shops and even breweries. However, as the photograph of Christabel Pankhurst on page 48 shows, women did not always attend. By the beginning of the twentieth century both the WSPU and the NUWSS were even holding meetings at fairs and wakes to publicise the cause. One of the most important meetings held by the WSPU took place in London. On February 13th 1907 the WSPU held what they called the first Women's Parliament at Caxton Hall, just across the square from the House of Commons, as a protest against their exclusion from the franchise. Suffrage meetings such as these often attracted large audiences. In 1880, one suffrage speaker filled the Manchester Free Trade Hall with women who had walked up to twenty miles to attend, as did Emmeline Pankhurst when she spoke there many years later.

Some considered these early suffragists daring and unladylike because it was unseemly for women to speak in public. Victorian society was profoundly shocked when Millicent Fawcett and another suffragist spoke to a mixed audience at the Architectural Society in London in 1869. One MP even mentioned the incident in Parliament: he referred to two ladies who had recently disgraced themselves but would not mention their names in case it caused further embarrassment. However, by the end of the nineteenth century public speaking had generally become unexceptional unless it took place at an unusual event. For instance, in 1908, when Millicent Fawcett became the first woman to debate at the Oxford Union she once again received a lot of publicity.

Christabel Pankhurst at an election meeting

b) Demonstrations and Pilgrimages

Demonstrations, a typical expression of protest by pressure groups, were common to all the suffrage organisations because they could draw members together in a feeling of communal identity, engender a sense of purpose and publicise votes for women. The first of the big suffrage demonstrations, organised by the NUWSS, took place in February 1907 and became known as the Mud March because of the torrential rain which poured down on the demonstrators. Even as late as 1907 it was considered unladylike to participate in outdoor protest, so the 3,000 or more women who marched from Hyde Park Corner risked their reputation and sometimes their employment. However, despite the rain, the demonstration was considered a great success, and so similar processions, which seemed to grow bigger by the year, were organised. One of the largest demonstrations took place on a Sunday in 1908 when several processions from half a dozen venues attracted more than 25,000 women. In 1911 a London march, held in honour of the new King George V, was organised by all the suffrage societies and drew approximately 40,000 demonstrators. A month long pilgrimage from Edinburgh to London in 1912 also drew thousands of supporters. Similarly a pilgrimage in August 1913 organised by the NUWSS (from all parts of Britain to the capital city) enjoyed great success. Demonstrators were greeted by bands and provided with food and drink throughout their journeys.

The WSPU gave demonstrations a new direction as, with impressive skill, they introduced a touch of melodrama to an old form of protest. The members of the WSPU were great show people who livened up demonstrations by making them into dramatic performances. As Diane Atkinson[2] has pointed out, the black and white photographs of this period do not reveal the fact that the movement was extremely colourful. When Emmeline Pethick Lawrence selected the colours of purple for dignity, white for purity and green for hope to represent the suffragettes, she created a vivid image. Suffragettes proudly wore these colours in public. They certainly dressed up for demonstrations: in plain white with sashes of purple, white and green; in the costumes of famous women (Joan of Arc was a popular figure); in their working clothes (as pit brow women, factory workers, doctors, teachers); in their national costume or carrying national flags (Scottish women wore tartan, Irish women carried flags and were accompanied by Irish pipers); and as ex-prisoners (dressed in prison clothes). Demonstrators carried eight feet high banners and enormous posters with the portraits of the leadership on them. Various bands, playing protest songs, accompanied these bright and dazzling processions. Hence one historian has called these events 'the spectacle of women'.

c) Propaganda Techniques

Throughout this period, all the various suffrage groups waged an intensive propaganda campaign to promote votes for women. They published their own newspapers and wrote their own plays, short stories and poems. The regular production of suffrage newspapers, such as *The Women's Suffrage Journal* from 1870 and *Votes for Women* from 1907, proved to be a valuable means of both publicising the women's suffrage cause and of keeping the various groups and associations in touch with one another.

The Actresses' Franchise League wrote and performed numerous propaganda plays in drawing rooms and public theatres in order to strengthen supporters and make converts. In these plays, the female was generally portrayed as a heroine pitted against an unyielding and intransigent male. One popular play called *The Reforming of Augustus*, concerned the conversion of an antagonistic male to women's suffrage as a result of a dream. Plays such as *How the Vote Was Won* written by Elizabeth Robins, an active member of the WSPU, were performed to sympathetic audiences throughout Britain.

Suffragettes even disrupted plays about female heroines. On one occasion three suffragettes barricaded themselves into a box at Covent Garden to interrupt the play *Joan of Arc*. These militants drew similarities between the treatment of Joan and the treatment of the suffragettes at the hands of a hostile government. A film called *True Womanhood*, which was about the struggle for women's suffrage, was produced and shown in cinemas. Music, poetry and limericks were also used to make the political point. *The March of the Women*, the rallying song for the WSPU, had a catchy tune and memorable lyrics. On the 10th February 1911 a poem entitled 'Woman This, and Woman That', written by Laurence Housman, was recited outside Woolwich Town Hall to an audience of hundreds:

1 We went before a magistrate who would not hear us speak;
To a drunken brute who beat his wife he only gave a week:
But we were sent to Holloway a calendar month or more,
Because we dared, against his will, to knock at Asquith's door.

5 When women go to work for them the Government engage
To give them lots of contract jobs at a low starvation wage;
But when it's men that they employ they always add a note -
'Fair wages must be paid' - because the men have got the vote.

You talk of sanitation, and temperance, and schools,
10 And you send your male inspectors to impose your man-made rules;
'The woman's sphere's the home' you say? then prove it to our face;
Give us the vote that we may make the home a happier place!

The WSPU, as Diane Atkinson has pointed out, were great saleswomen. They designed, advertised and marketed a wide variety of goods in their London shops. Tea Caddies, soap, cakes and even the ubiquitous stock cube were designed for sale in the suffragette colours. Cards, crackers, jewellery, suffragette dolls, scarves in various shades of purple, white summer blouses, badges, bags and belts were all sold in the WSPU shops. Books, pamphlets and leaflets, stationery, games and playing cards were also on display. Bazaars were organised to raise money and to promote support. At one bazaar in Glasgow, which raised over £1,700, a quilt embroidered with the names of suffragette hunger strikers was offered for sale. At the Women's Exhibition and Sale of Work in Knightsbridge in 1909 a photographic history of the suffrage movement, a reproduction of a prison cell, plays performed by the Actresses Franchise League entertained - and educated - the vast numbers who attended. In the two weeks in which the exhibition was open it collected £6,000 and recruited over 200 women.

Some of the methods used in the early twentieth century, particularly by the WSPU, suggest a playfulness and sense of humour that was far removed from the conventional dour image of the suffrage movement. The WSPU was highly innovative in its propaganda techniques, rarely missing an opportunity to promote votes for women. Groups of cyclists went out regularly on bicycles decorated with the suffragette colours to advertise demonstrations. At the 1908 Football Cup Final, held at Crystal Palace in London, the WSPU distributed envelopes with the teams' colours on them inviting the wives of the male spectators to meetings. On the day of the match they flew a kite with 'Votes for Women' written on it above the pitch and distributed suffragette leaflets at nearby railway stations. At one of the boat races between Oxford and Cambridge, the WSPU ran a launch filled with 'Votes for Women' banners, while on another occasion it hired a boat to sail to the House of Commons in order to harangue MPs taking tea on the terrace. One member of the Women's Freedom League even hired a balloon to fly across London to drop leaflets supporting votes for women.

d) Persuading Parliament

As only Parliament had the constitutional right to grant the vote to women, suffragists tried desperately to convince MPs of the logic of women's suffrage. At first, conventional middle-class methods of pressure were used: the legality of women's exclusion from the vote was tested; Parliament was petitioned and MPs were lobbied. It was the politics of persuasion rather than the politics of confrontation. However, peaceful protests were superseded by violence when Parliament refused to budge. By 1914 the suffragettes increasingly favoured intimidating methods, whereas the suffragists continued to exert, what was now deemed, moderate pressure.

In the 1860s suffragists attempted to use the legal system to gain the vote. They alleged that women had once enjoyed the right to vote but had been excluded in 1832 when for the first time the Great Reform Act specified 'male' persons. They challenged the legality of the 1832 Reform Act in two cases: Chorlton *v.* Lings in England and Brown *v.* Ingram in Scotland but the suffragists lost their case when the Courts refused to accept the validity of their claim (see page 10).

Petitioning the House of Commons was a time-honoured way of publicising reform issues: the Anti-Corn League had successfully used this method. It was favoured not only because it indicated to the Government that large numbers were in favour of votes for women but because it helped arouse public interest in the campaign. But because women were without the vote their petitions were not viewed as sympathetically as those of the men who petitioned against the Corn Laws of the early nineteenth century.

Suffragists also lobbied MPs to gain their support for women's suffrage. In June 1887 Lydia Becker formed the first Committee of Members of Parliament who pledged their commitment to votes for women. Seventy-one MPs joined. As a result of the combined work of this Committee and the NUWSS, a private member's bill in support of women's suffrage was brought in almost every year. Efforts were also made to amend government franchise bills to include women's suffrage. In 1867, the great philosopher, John Stuart Mill introduced the first ever women's suffrage amendment to the Second Reform Bill while William Woodall, a Liberal MP for Stoke on Trent, tried to secure the inclusion of a woman's suffrage amendment to the Third Reform Bill of 1884. The three Plural voting Bills of 1906, 1913 and 1914 and the 1912 Irish Home Rule Bill each had an amendment attached in support of votes for women. All of the amendments failed.

In the late nineteenth and early twentieth century suffragists worked hard to elect Liberal MPs who supported votes for women. It was common practice for the NUWSS to canvass votes for sympathetic Liberal MPs at general elections and by-elections. For instance in the 1910 general election the Birmingham branch of the NUWSS wrote to 52 parliamentary candidates to obtain their views on women's suffrage, undertook door-to-door canvassing to support sympathisers and picketed the election booths. In 1906 Wigan textile workers canvassed at by-elections for MPs who supported women's suffrage and in 1907 the NUWSS adopted a similar approach in Hexham, Jarrow, Kirkdale and Wimbledon. In Wimbledon the NUWSS ran the entire election campaign of the women's suffrage candidate.

Until the Liberal landslide of 1906 the NUWSS concentrated much of its energies on opposing Conservative candidates. However, the Liberal victory left the NUWSS with a political dilemma. Although the Liberals brought women's suffrage no further forward, suffragists had no wish to embarrass a government which so many of them supported and to which many of their male relatives belonged. By 1910, however, the patience of the NUWSS had worn thin and it became official

NUWSS policy to run suffrage candidates against opponents from all of the major political parties, including the Liberals.

From 1912 onwards the NUWSS, disillusioned by what they perceived as the continuing duplicity of the Liberal Party, redirected its allegiance to the Labour Party. It subsidised Labour MPs in Parliament who were sympathetic to women's suffrage and set up an Election Fighting Fund to sustain Labour candidates and to defeat the Liberals. These tactics were thought to be successful. In the last by-election campaign supported by the Election Fighting Fund, fought in Midlothian Scotland in 1912, the NUWSS claimed that the Liberals had been defeated because their Labour candidate had taken away valuable Liberal votes.

Nonetheless, despite the efforts of both the suffragists and the suffragettes, votes for women seemed no further forward. As a consequence, the suffragettes turned to other forms of political action to get their voice heard. And it is this type of action which has aroused the most controversy.

3 Illegal Methods

The popular image of the militant is of a woman chained to railings outside government offices shouting 'Votes for Women'. In fact, the first illegal methods used by the suffragists and suffragettes were little more than mild forms of civil disobedience. At first women tried to undermine the business of the government by refusing to support a state that refused them recognition. Two of the most common ways to achieve this were tax and census evasion.

a) Tax Evasion and Census Resistance

The refusal of women to pay their taxes had a long history in the annals of the suffrage movement, as women very early on claimed that taxation and representation were inseparably united (see page 12). In 1870 two Quaker suffragists, who refused to pay taxes, had their property seized by bailiffs. More than 35 years later Mrs Montefiore barricaded herself in her Hammersmith house in defiance of the bailiffs sent to seize her home in lieu of tax payments. The Women's Freedom League, under the direction of Charlotte Despard, adopted a similar policy and described it as 'constitutional militancy'. A number of wealthy suffragists lost property and faced heavy fines for non payment of taxes but continued to believe that the sacrifice was worthwhile.

All the suffrage groups linked the census with citizenship and citizenship with suffrage so that 'no-vote, no-census' became one of their rallying cries. Every ten years, since 1801, the government organised an official count of the population - a census - in order to plan for the future. The Women's Freedom League organised a boycott of the 1911 census, and this was endorsed by the WSPU and the NUWSS. On

April 2nd 1911, the day of the census, large numbers of women made elaborate arrangements to be away from home for the night in order to avoid the census enumerator. Women with large houses offered overnight accommodation. In Edinburgh a large cafe was hired by the WSPU so that women who wanted to evade the census had somewhere safe to stay overnight. Others stayed in the WFL headquarters in Glasgow or the WSPU offices elsewhere, some went to the all night entertainments put on by the various suffrage societies; and at least one member of the WFL spent the whole night on roller skates at the Aldwych Skating Rink!

b) Reasons for Increased Militancy

From 1908 the WSPU intensified the political pressure and promoted new and confrontational methods to force MPs to give women the vote. The reason for this turn to violence is open to debate. Unsympathetic observers have viewed militancy humourously or else sought explanations within a psychological framework of madness and abnormality. George Dangerfield, for example, writes comically about women:

1   It is almost impossible to write the story of the Woman's Rebellion without admitting certain elements of brutal comedy. From the spectacle of women attacking men there rises an outrageous, an unprincipled laughter. And when a scene as ordinary as English politics is suddenly disturbed with the swish of long skirts, the violent
5   assault of feathered hats, the impenetrable, advancing phalanx of corseted bosoms - when, around the smoking ruins of some house or church, there is discovered the dread evidence of a few hairpins or a feminine galosh - then the amazing, the ludicrous appearance of the whole thing is almost irresistible.[3]

Militancy, for some anti-suffragists, was seen as a reflection of the widespread instability of women, and of fanatical and hysterical women more particularly. Hence, to them, it was proof that women should not be allowed to vote. The first historians to write about the suffragettes agreed with the anti-suffragists, emphasised the psychological weakness of the suffragettes and decried militancy as the action of a few demented spinsters. Some saw militancy as the sign of 'individual psychological imbalance'[4]. whereas others viewed it an expression of a malaise affecting women more broadly. Recently, however, historians are critical of this interpretation and suggest that militancy was a rational response to male intransigence. Brian Harrison[5], for example, claims that militancy was a temporary tactical necessity born of the failure of legal and peaceful methods. Even so Harrison is not averse to trivialising the women's struggle:'This inversion of society's values was by no means complete; it closely resembles the schoolgirls' surreptitious breaking of the rules when the headmistress is away rather than

the revolutionary's contemptuous and frontal challenge to the established order.'[6] Radical feminist historians view suffragette violence
quite differently. To their minds, violent behaviour challenged male
supremacy, thus establishing the WSPU as not only heroic but as the
precursor of modern feminism. Radical feminists may well take the
violence of the WSPU seriously but the adoption of a Whiggish interpretation (whereby the WSPU is seen to have lain the foundation for
women's emancipation) needs to be queried.

Suffragettes did not offer such a psychological interpretation of
their behaviour but argued that violence emerged, and escalated, for
a number of strategic reasons. Firstly, militancy was adopted in
response to the failure of years of peaceful campaigning to which
politicians were seen to have turned a deaf ear. Secondly, militancy
was a reaction to the 1906 Liberal Government which, by excluding
women from public meetings and refusing to meet suffrage deputations, had denied suffragettes the main forms of agitation open to the
disenfranchised. Forbidden access to peaceful protest, suffragettes
believed that they were left with only one alternative: violence.
Thirdly, militancy was seen as a retaliatory measure against a
Government which imprisoned and force-fed those who participated
in direct action (see pages 75-6). If the Government chose to treat
women roughly then it too would be intimidated. Fourthly,
suffragettes believed themselves to be continuing a long and vener-
able tradition of protest as previous extensions to the franchise, for
instance in 1832 and 1867, had been preceded by great disturbances.
The WSPU drew on historical examples of the unlawful exercise of
physical force to justify its tactics and identified the suffragettes with
past revolutionary and resistance heroes. One male supporter of votes
for women remarked ironically:

> 1 Of course, when men wanted the franchise, they did not behave in
>   the unruly manner of our feminine friends. They were perfectly
>   constitutional in their agitation. In Bristol, I find they only burnt the
>   Mansion House, the Custom House, the Bishop's Palace, the Excise
>   Office, three prisons, four tollhouses, and forty-two private dwellings
> 5 and warehouses, all in a perfectly constitutional and respectable
>   manner ... Four men were respectably hanged at Bristol and three
>   in Nottingham ... In this and other ways the males set a splendid
>   example of constitutional methods in agitating for the franchise.[7]

Finally, suffragettes were persuaded that the Government would not
grant women the vote until they were forced to do so. Comparisons
were drawn between the suffragettes and other pressure groups who
advocated violent methods. Christabel Pankhurst, for instance, noted
that miners had succeeded in gaining improved pay and conditions in
1911 because they made themselves a nuisance. Similarly the tactics of
the Ulster Unionists, seen to go unchecked and unpunished even
when it involved the loss of human life, were successful in stopping

the move towards Irish Home Rule. The suffragettes believed that the achievements of these groups demonstrated that the vote would only be obtained through violent action.

It is often assumed that this kind of behaviour was orchestrated by the iconoclastic WSPU leadership who marshalled their obedient membership to commit crimes. Militancy, however, often began at a local level with a few ardent activists and was only adopted as WSPU policy when it received extensive support from the membership. As Sandra Holton has pointed out, window smashing, arson, letter burning and hunger striking were all initiated by rank and file members. Indeed, there is evidence to suggest, that rather than encourage impetuous behaviour, the WSPU leadership tried to restrain the enthusiasms of its rank and file for ever-increasing violent tactics.

c) Window Smashing

One of the first violent tactics of the WSPU was breaking windows: an impromptu act borne of desperation rather than a coherent political strategy. The first window smashing began as a response to the treatment that women received outside the House of Commons in 1908. Asquith, the Prime Minister, had refused to receive a deputation of suffragettes who were subsequently treated with great brutality. Exasperated, Edith New and Mary Leigh smashed two windows at 10 Downing Street.

The next bout of window smashing occurred when Emmeline Pankhurst and a group of elderly suffragists were evicted from the House of Commons and arrested when trying to deliver a petition. This event prompted women to break windows at the Privy Council, the Treasury and the Home Office in protest against such treatment. Once again, window breaking was not authorised by the WSPU leadership but was an angry and impassioned response to government intransigence and police violence. Yet window breaking soon gained retrospective approval from the leadership of the WSPU, and then it became official policy. When Mrs Pankhurst remarked that 'the argument of the broken window pane is the most valuable argument in modern politics', it gave licence to the window smashers. Soon after, this window smashing became part of a well orchestrated campaign, with suffragettes travelling down from as far as Scotland to take part.[8] Even so, window smashing generally occurred not haphazardly but as a consequence of alleged government double-dealing. For instance, when Asquith rejected a Conciliation Bill for women's suffrage in November 1911 the WSPU responded with violence immediately and shattered windows at the Home Office, the War Office, the Foreign Office, the Board of Education, the Board of Trade, the Treasury, Somerset House, The National Liberal Club, Guards Club, the *Daily Mail* and the *Daily News*.

On another occasion, when a Liberal Cabinet Minister commented that the women's suffrage movement had not generated the kind of popular uprising associated with previous pressure groups, the suffragettes responded by an unprecedented day of destruction. On March 1st 1912, *The Times* reported that groups of fashionably dressed women smashed windows in the Strand, in Cockspur Street, in the Haymarket, and Piccadilly, in Coventry Street, in Regent Street, in part of Oxford Street and in Bond Street. Apparently, the attack was made simultaneously in the different streets, and in spite of the amount of damage done the whole disturbance only extended over a comparatively short period.

d) Arson Attacks

Arson attacks, like window breaking, were initially advanced by individuals acting on their own initiative and only later became official WSPU policy. Emily Davison's destruction of a pillar box in December 1911 shifted militancy on to a new level, especially when endorsed by speeches by Emmeline Pankhurst, who said at the Albert Hall in October 1912:

1 Those of you who can express your militancy by facing Party mobs at Cabinet Ministers' meetings when you remind them of their falseness to principle - do so. Those of you who can express your militancy by joining us in our anti-Government by-election policy - do so. Those of you who can break windows - break them. Those of
5 you who can still further attack the secret idol of property so as to make the Government realise that property is as greatly endangered by Women Suffrage as it was by the Chartists of old - do so. And my last word to the Government: I cite this meeting to rebellion. You have not dared to take the leaders of Ulster for their incitement to
10 rebellion, take me if you dare.

Although there were a few sporadic arson attacks before 1913 the partial destruction of Lloyd George's country house in Surrey that year marked a watershed in suffragette violence. 'We have tried blowing him up to wake his conscience,' said Emmeline Pankhurst.[9] Many of the arson attacks were, like window smashing, a response to particular political events. At least four of the major acts of arson committed in March 1914 were precipitated by the arrests of Emmeline Pankhurst. In Ireland, violent action, such as destroying the windows of English-owned buildings like Dublin Castle, was almost always in response to the failure of a women's suffrage amendment in England. The arson campaign was widespread throughout Britain as you can see from 'A Year's Record' on page 58.

258 THE SUFFRAGETTE December 26, 1913.

A YEAR'S RECORD.

The following are the more serious attacks on property which have been attributed to Suffragettes during the year 1913.

January 13.—Estimate that women have broken glass worth from £1,000 to £5,000.

January 28.—Women sentenced for damaging Windsor Castle. Fifty women arrested for window-smashing in West End of London.

January 30.—Windows of Lambeth Palace broken.

February 3.—Case smashed in jewelroom at Tower of London.

February 8.—Hundreds of orchids destroyed at Kew Gardens.

February 12.—Kiosk burnt in Regent's Park: damage £400.

February 16.—Wholesale raid on golf links, many greens being damaged.

February 17.—Great Central Railway carriage fired at Harrow.

February 19.—House building for Mr. Lloyd George blown up at Walton Heath.

March 10.—Saunderton and Croxley Green stations destroyed by fire.

March 11.—Revolver shots and vitriol thrown at Nottingham Suffragette meeting.

March 16.—£2,000 house burnt at Cheam.

March 20.—Lady White's house, Staines, burnt down; £3,000 damage.

March 24.—House set on fire at Beckenham.

March 27.—House fired at Hampstead: petrol explosion.

April 2.—Church fired at Hampstead Garden Suburb.

April 3.—Four houses fired at Hampstead Garden Suburb.

April 4.—Mansion near Chorley Wood destroyed by fire; bomb explosion at Oxted Station; empty train wrecked by bomb explosion at Devonport; famous pictures damaged at Manchester.

April 5.—Ayr racecourse stand burnt : £3,000 damage; attempt to destroy Kelso racecourse grand stand.

April 6.—House fired at Potter's Bar; mansion destroyed at Norwich.

April 8.—Plot to destroy Crystal Palace stands before the Football Cup tie.

April 8.—Explosion in grounds of Dudley Castle; bomb found in heavily-laden Kingston train at Queen's Road, Battersea.

April 11.—Tunbridge Wells cricket pavilion destroyed.

April 12.—Council schools, Gateshead, set on fire.

April 15.—Mansion fired at St. Leonard's; damage £9,000; Home Office order prohibits Suffragette meetings.

April 19.—Attempt to wreck Smeaton's famous Eddystone Lighthouse on Plymouth Hoe.

April 20.—Attempt to blow up offices of "York Herald," York, with a bomb.

April 23.—Attempt to burn Minster Church, Isle of Thanet.

April 24.—Bomb explodes at County Council offices, Newcastle.

April 26.—Railway carriage destroyed by fire at Teddington.

April 30.—Boathouse burned at Hampton Court : £3,500 damage; Suffragettes' headquarters seized by police, five leaders arrested.

May 1. Buildings burned at Hendon.

May 3.—Amazing Suffragette plots disclosed at Bow Street.

May 6.—Woman Suffrage Bill defeated in Commons; St. Catherine's Church, Hatcham, burned down.

May 7. Bomb found in St. Paul's Cathedral; two bungalows damaged near Bexhill; bowlinggreen chalet, Bishop's Park, Fulham, destroyed.

May 9. Oaklea, near Barrow, fired.

May 10. Farringdon Hall, Dundee, destroyed : damage £10,000; private house, Beckenham, fired.

May 12. Boathouse on the Trent destroyed : damage nearly £2,000.

May 13. Private house, Hendon, badly destroyed.

May 14.—Private house Folkestone, fired : damage from £700 to £1,000; Penn Church damaged.

May 15.—St. Anne's Church, Eastbourne, damaged.

May 18.—Parish Rooms, St. Anne's, Eastbourne, damaged by fire; private house, Cambridge, destroyed by fire : damage between £700 to £1,000; buildings belonging to University, Cambridge, damaged.

May 21.—Bomb explosion, Blackford Observatory, Edinburgh : serious damage.

May 22.—Trinity Wesleyan Church, Stamford, burned; stables, Stamford Hotel, damaged.

May 23.—South Bromley Station damaged by fire.

May 28.—Good's Yard, G.C. Railway Station, Nottingham, timber stacks destroyed.

May 31.—Shields Road Station, Glasgow, damaged.

June 3.—Rough's boathouse, Oxford, destroyed : damage £3,000; Westwood Manor, Trowbridge, destroyed by fire : damage £15,000.

June 7.—North Middlesex Cricket Club pavilion destroyed by fire : business premises at Bradford destroyed : damage £80,000.

June 11.—Private house, East Lothian, destroyed : damage £7,000.

June 12.—Assembly Rooms and Pier Hotel, Withernsea, destroyed.

June 13.—Eden Park Station damaged; three further outbreaks in Bradford.

June 18.—Rowley Regis Church, near Dudley, destroyed : damage £6,000.

June 19.—Private house, Olton, destroyed.

June 21.—Gatty Marine Laboratory, St. Andrew's University, partially destroyed.

June 25.—Hazlewell Railway Station damaged.

June 30.—Ballikinian Castle, Stirlingshire, destroyed : damage £70,000; Lencross Railway Station destroyed : damage £2,000.

July 4.—Private house, South Coldfiels, destroyed : damage £4,000.

July 8.—Sir W. Lever's bungalow destroyed.

July 21.—Private house, Perry Bar, damaged.

August 4.—Private house, Woldingham, damaged.

August 5.—Holiday House, Lyton, destroyed : damage £10,000; motor car burned.

August 8.—School, Sutton-in-Ashfield, damaged; private house, Finchley : damage £500; hayricks fired, Abergavenny : damage £50.

August 13.—Laxey Glen Pavilion, Isle of Man, destroyed : damage £5,000.

August 14.—Carnarvon School House damaged.

August 15.—Haystacks burned near Liverpool : damage £350; Willesden Park pavilion destroyed : damage £250.

August 16.—Private house, Bangor, damaged.

August 19.—Bedford Timber Yard : damage £200.

August 22.—Private house, Edinburgh : damage £300; Fettes College, Edinburgh, damaged.

August 23.—Haystacks burned Littlemore, Burnham Beeches, and Maltby : damage about £300; motor cars burned at Hunsworth, Birmingham.

September 1.—Bomb found in Cheltenham Town Hall; house fired at Newcastle; school fired at Oldbury; International Correspondence Schools fired at Finchley.

September 5.—Fire at Dulwich College : damage £300.

September 11.—Stanstead House, Seaton, fired : damage £500.

September 13.—Kenton House gutted : damage £1,000.

September 16.—Wheat rick destroyed at Berkhampstead; Penlurst Place burnt.

September 19.—House fired at Finchley; house fired at Liverpool.

September 23.—Seafield House, Derby, completely gutted : damage £80,000.

September 22.—Withernsea Town Hall gutted; The Cedars, Waltham Cross, destroyed by fire; fire at Warren Hill, Longton.

September 27.—Fire at timber yards, Yarmouth : damage £40,000.

September 28.—Fire at Frensham Hall, Farnham; Football Ground stand at Plumstead destroyed by fire : damage £1,000; hayricks fired near Oldbury : damage £200.

October 2.—Hayricks and farm fired at Willesden.

October 4.—The Elms, Hampton-on-Thames burnt out : damage £3,000.

October 7.—Two houses fired at Bedford.

October 10.—Yarmouth Pier fired.

October 12.—Wrighley Head Mill, Failsworth, fired.

October 19.—Red House, Loughborough, fired.

October 23.—Bristol Line Athletic Ground destroyed by fire : damage £2,200.

October 22.—Two stations in Birmingham fired.

October 26.—Brooklands, Farnham Royal, destroyed by fire.

October 28.—Shirley Manor, Wyke, completely destroyed by fire : damage £5,000; Mill House, Bramshill, destroyed by fire; Station fired at Oldbury.

November 2.—Streatham Station fired.

November 8.—Stockton Grand Stand fired.

November 11.—Bomb explosion in Cactus House, Alexandra Park, Manchester : damage to glass alone £200; Begbrook, Bristol, fired : damage £3,000; Bowling Green Club pavilion at Catford burned to ground : damage £1,500.

November 15.—Bomb found in Palm House, Sefton Park, Liverpool.

November 16.—The Priory, Sandown Park, Liverpool : three floors and roof destroyed.

November 17.—Newton Road Station, Birmingham, fired.

November 20.—Mill at Ashton-under-Lyne fired : damage £200; fire at timber yard, Oxford : damage £3,000.

November 22.—Football Stand, Blackburn, fired.

November 23.—Bristol boathouse burned : damage £300.

November 24.—Castle Bromwich Station fired.

November 27.—Caerleon Training College, Newport, fired : damage £10,000.

November 24.—Hurstfield, hayricks burned : damage £2,000.

December 5.—Kelly House, Wemyss Bay, fired : damage £60,000.

December 6.—Rusholme Exhibition, Manchester, fired : damage £12,000; Liverpool Exhibition fired.

December 13.—Scottish mansion (Ardgare) fired : damage £10,000.

December 15.—Devonport timber yards fired, more than £2,000 damage; Bristol mansion burnt.

December 16.—Liverpool church fired.

December 18.—Explosion at Holloway Prison.

MRS. PANKHURST'S LICENCE.

Readers are asked to note that Mrs. Pankhurst's last licence is on sale for the highest bidder.

A year's record of Suffragette activity

e) Other Damaging Behaviour

Suffragettes also tried to destroy valuable works of art as a protest against the higher value placed on property than people. The most famous case was Mary Richardson, who attacked with an axe the painting of Venus by Velasquez which hung in the National Gallery. Mary Richardson, later known as 'Slasher Mary', wanted to draw a parallel between the public's indifference to Emmeline Pankhurst's health and their respect for a valuable object, saying that 'You can get another picture, but you cannot get a life, as they are killing Mrs Pankhurst.'[10] (Emmeline Pankhurst was very weak at this time due to constant imprisonment and hunger striking.) Other suffragettes used similar tactics. In the same year, a woman spoiled a painting by Romney which hung in Birmingham Art Gallery, while another tried to mutilate the picture of the King in the Royal Scottish Academy. The WSPU also cut telegraph wires, wrecked plants in Kew Greenhouse and burnt messages with acid into golf courses saying 'No Votes, No Golf'. Yet, perhaps the greatest damage the suffragettes did was to themselves. The best known and the most tragic incident involved Emily Davison who died accidentally as a result of injuries sustained at the 1913 Derby. She was not the only one to die in the suffrage cause: Ellen Pitfield died of incurable injuries received on Black Friday 1910 (see page 73). Many others, including Lady Constance Lytton who suffered a stroke in 1912, were physically weakened as a result of their suffrage activities and died at an early age.

These particular law breaking activities were well orchestrated and more reminiscent of guerrilla warfare than traditional forms of political protest. In Scotland, for example, pillar box attacks were organised with great precision. Activists met at a pre-arranged time and place to be handed bottles of acid, which had usually been obtained by sympathetic chemist members, and told exactly when to drop them into pillar boxes for the greatest effect. In activities such as these the suffragettes tried to remain anonymous: one activist always dressed as a domestic servant, with black dress and white muslin apron, to avoid suspicion.

f) Hunger Striking

By engaging in illegal activities, the suffragettes were liable to arrest and imprisonment; once imprisoned, large numbers went on hunger strike as a protest against unfair detention and to gain publicity. As with the first window smashers and the first arsonists, the first hunger striker, Marion Wallace-Dunlop, conceived of the idea independently when imprisoned for stencilling a quotation from the Bill of Rights on a wall in the House of Commons. This action soon become official WSPU policy especially as hunger strikers were released from prison when their health was seen to be in danger.

The WSPU used the experiences of hunger strikers to gain widespread sympathy. Stories regularly appeared in *Votes for Women* about the way in which women were brutally treated. The paper drew attention to the class differences within prison by informing readers that when working-class women were forcibly fed they were not given any medical aid or examined to see if they were fit. Selina Martin, a working-class woman arrested in Liverpool, was kept in chains and frog-marched to her cell. In contrast, upper- and middle-class women were given preferential treatment and shown greater consideration. These discrepancies prompted Lady Constance Lytton, in 1911, to disguise herself as a working-class woman called Jane Wharton to commit a criminal act and face arrest and imprisonment. As Lady Constance Lytton, she had always been medically examined and found unfit to be force-fed. As Jane Wharton she received no such care and was brutally force-fed seven times. This case attracted much publicity and enabled the WSPU to draw attention to the class distinctions which existed both in prison and the wider society and which the female vote might help to eliminate.

Historians have often dealt with the women's prison experiences and particularly the hunger strikes in a decidedly unsympathetic manner. George Dangerfield, for example, insinuates that the suffragettes were masochists who enjoyed the experience of imprisonment, for 'how can one avoid the thought that they sought these sufferings with an enraptured, a positively unhealthy pleasure?'[11] In contrast, radical feminists such as Jane Marcus believe that hunger striking should be seen as a political act performed by committed activists rather than the actions of an unstable person.

g) Harassing Authority

The WSPU directed its energies towards disrupting what they regarded as the male authority of church and state. The Church was singled out as an object of attack because it was seen paradoxically both as the 'lackey' of government and as a symbol of resistance against authority (see pages 78-9 for the church response to the suffrage movement). Either way, the suffragettes showed remarkable religious dedication. On the one hand, the Church was condemned for its 'shameful and obsequiously compliant attitude'[12] in not speaking out against the perceived torture of imprisoned suffragette martyrs. Yet, on the other hand, the church was criticised because it denied the Christian doctrine of equality by not actively supporting votes for women. And largely because Jesus Christ was regarded as a rebel who spoke out against injustice, the church was thought to need reminding of its historical role in championing the oppressed. There were therefore widespread protests in various churches and cathedrals where suffragettes interrupted services to pray in support of votes for women. For example, in 1913 at St Mary's Baptist Chapel in

Norwich a woman rose during the service to say 'Oh Lord Jesus, who dost at all times show tender compassion to women, hear now our petitions for our sisters who are being tortured in prison ... by men calling themselves Christians.'[13] Annie Kenney even arrived with her luggage at Lambeth Palace to seek sanctuary from the Archbishop of Canterbury until the vote had been won, but after providing her with lunch and tea he called the police who arrested her instead.

Only Parliament, however, had the authority to grant the vote to women and so the WSPU focused most of their attention there. Almost from the very beginning the WSPU heckled MPs because politicians had ignored their gentle persuasive tactics. The first incident occurred in 1905 during an election campaign when Christabel Pankhurst and Annie Kenney interrupted Sir Edward Grey and Winston Churchill at a meeting in Manchester's Free Trade Hall. During a pause in questions, Annie Kenney asked Churchill 'If you are elected, will you do your best to make Women's Suffrage a Government measure?' When no reply was given, Christabel Pankhurst held up a banner entitled 'Votes for Women'. At this moment, the lecture theatre erupted and when order was restored the Chief Constable of Manchester suggested putting the question in writing. Edward Grey and Churchill, both of whom paid lip service to women's suffrage, refused to answer the question. Just as the meeting was to be adjourned Annie Kenney unfurled a banner asking for votes for women and shouted 'Will the Liberal Government give women the vote?' The banner display and Annie Kenney's interruption caused further uproar and stewards and police evicted the two women from the hall. In response, Christabel Pankhurst spat in the face of at least two police officers and hit another. When Christabel and Annie Kenney attempted to address the crowd which had assembled outside the Hall, they were arrested and eventually fined and charged with disorderly behaviour and obstruction. Christabel Pankhurst used the subsequent trial as a political platform stating that 'we cannot make any orderly protest because we have not the means whereby citizens may do such a thing; we have not a vote; and so long as we have not votes we must be disorderly'. They refused to pay the fine - or even accept the payment of the fine by Winston Churchill - and so were imprisoned.

This incident created what Christabel Pankhurst desired: much needed publicity for women's suffrage. Imprisonment was news. Protests at public meetings addressed by members of the Government proved to be a very successful means of calling attention to the demand for votes for women. A meeting (in the same Hall) organised by the WSPU to welcome the return of the militants was packed to capacity. The two who had been unceremoniously thrown out a week previously were now on the platform speaking to an audience prepared to listen carefully to what they had to say. Despite criticism from the press about the unladylike behaviour of Annie Kenney and Christabel Pankhurst, the WSPU began to attract vast audiences and perhaps, more importantly, enjoyed an increase in membership.

This sequence of events was to be re-enacted again and again as women interrupted government leaders, were arrested, refused to pay fines and were imprisoned and then received what was in essence free publicity and as a consequence increased membership. It was a heady formula for success. All the leaders of the Liberal Party - Churchill, Campbell-Bannerman, Asquith, Lloyd George and Edward Grey - suffered from WSPU heckling at their meetings, whether they supported women's suffrage or not. At first it was just the Liberal Party which suffered from interruptions, but in October 1912 the WSPU decided to oppose Labour Party MPs at by-elections because they had pledged support to a Liberal government which force-fed women. The WSPU even interrupted political speeches when Liberal MPs were talking in support of women's suffrage because its leaders believed that these politicians were insincere. For example, Winston Churchill had his speeches interrupted because, as a senior member of the Liberal Government, he was held equally responsible for its refusal to grant women the vote. Similarly, in 1908 Lloyd George was heckled by WSPU members wearing prison uniforms when he gave a speech to a women's suffrage meeting sponsored by the WFL. This policy sometimes had even odder results. In a by-election in Dumfries the Liberal candidate, who supported women's suffrage, gained help from the NUWSS but was opposed and heckled by the WSPU because he represented the government in power.

When the government responded by banning women from political meetings the WSPU proved to be ingenious. Suffragettes concealed themselves between organ pipes, lurked under platforms or even arrived in mid air swinging on ropes through skylights! When Churchill, MP for Dundee, was due to speak at the Kinnaird Hall in Dundee suffragettes concealed themselves in a building nearby so that they could throw stones at the windows in the skylight of the roof. Similarly, in Birmingham, two women climbed on the roof of a house to threw tiles on to Asquith, who was due to speak at a nearby hall. Politicians were also harassed at golf clubs, when they were leaving churches and when they were dining at home.

Jane Marcus stresses the importance of the 'interruption of male political discourse'[14] in the suffrage campaign. The strategy of interrupting the speeches of male politicians, she suggests, marked a watershed in suffrage history. By stopping male politicians speaking the suffragettes not only challenged male authority but claimed a political voice for women who were supposed to remain silent. Of course this is historical speculation: the WSPU perhaps had more pragmatic reasons for interrupting the Government. Indeed they were possibly more influenced by Parnell's obstructionist tactics in the Irish Home Rule campaign of the 1880s than in interrupting men to make a feminist point. Parnell heckled all Liberal candidates at elections whether or not they supported Home Rule because the

Liberal Government was held responsible for the continuing coloni-
sation of Ireland. The Pankhursts had a good sense of history and
were all too aware that Richard Pankhurst, who had stood for
Parliament as a Liberal candidate, had been defeated in 1885 because
of Irish opposition. If the WSPU could similarly embarrass the Liberal
Government then the vote would not be far off - or so it was thought.

4 Conclusion

Despite the large number of articles and books on the suffrage movement, the suffragists and the suffragettes have continued to be written
about as two separate groups. On the one side, the law-abiding constitutionalist organisations, such as the NUWSS, who advocated peaceful
persuasion; on the other side, the ungovernable WSPU who preferred
destruction to reason. However, it is important to remember that the
suffrage movement was one story with several subplots rather than
totally different sagas. After all, the suffrage organisations shared a
common goal - votes for women - and only differed on the ways to
achieve it. Perhaps it is only historians, desperate to tidy up the past
and impose an order on a rather chaotic movement, who need to
categorise the suffrage movement in such a linear way.

The destructive methods of the WSPU have been the subject of
much historical research. In 1860, when this story begins, only
peaceful methods were used, whereas by 1914 suffragette violence was
at its height. And it is this turn towards violence that has tended to
dominate the history texts. However, the WSPU did not break with the
suffragist past but built upon it; violent measures did not replace
constitutional ones so much as supplement them. Throughout this
whole period both the suffragists and suffragettes continued to use the
traditional forms of protest such as petitioning Parliament, lobbying
MPs and demonstrating. Furthermore, both the suffragists and the
suffragettes often tried to end the impasse between themselves and the
Liberal Government by supporting the two Conciliation Bills put
forward in the House of Commons to enfranchise women. On these
occasions all the suffrage organisations co-operated with each
Conciliation Committee which proposed the Bill. They lobbied MPs,
sent speakers to various organisations and directed local constituency
groups to pressurise MPs to vote for each Bill. And while negotiations
continued the WSPU called a truce. Both Conciliation Bills, as we
know, failed to become law. The defeat of each disillusioned the
suffrage groups: many NUWSS women resigned from the Liberal
Party, whereas the WSPU reverted to violence.

Nevertheless, there is no doubt that the NUWSS leaders, although
working towards the same goal, grew irritated by the increasingly
destructive tactics of the WSPU. Over the years, they had tried to
prove that they (and, by association, women in general) were calm,
sensible and rational beings and so they put forward measured argu-

ments and used democratic methods to get their message across. It was feared that the use of violence discredited the suffrage movement and undermined suffragist efforts to be seen as mature adults who could be trusted with the vote. However, the NUWSS leaders were reluctant to criticise the WSPU openly and publicly in case it added fuel to the Government fire of obstinacy.

The question whether the violence of the suffragettes was self-defeating is often asked. It is sometimes argued that it lost the WSPU the sympathy and support of the country at large and provided the Liberal Government with an ideal excuse to deny women the vote. Not surprisingly, the WSPU leaders denied the accusation that violence was counter-productive. On the contrary, to believe that militancy damaged the suffrage cause was to be ignorant of all the lessons taught by history. To their minds, persuasive tactics - not militant methods - were ineffective as the peaceful methods of the suffragists had brought the vote no further forward in 1905 (when militancy is said to have begun) than it had fifty years before. And so the WSPU, their patience exhausted, hoped to force the government into conceding votes for women by using the weapon of violence. Nevertheless, suffragette violence was still circumscribed by their ideological beliefs. Although they were prepared to sacrifice their own lives in the pursuit of votes for women, the suffragettes generally confined themselves to attacks on property rather than people. Certainly, up until 1914, when the WSPU ceased its campaigning, Cabinet Ministers and others were rarely in any personal danger because the WSPU stated that they held a scrupulous respect for human life. However, it is tempting to speculate whether this belief in the sacredness of human life would have lasted if war had not broken out as, after all, the suffragettes had already begun to throw slates and other missiles at government ministers.

References

1 Sandra Holton, *Feminism and Democracy* (Cambridge University Press, 1986).
2 Diane Atkinson, *Purple, White and Green* (Museum of London, 1992).
3 George Dangerfield, *The Strange Death of Liberal England* (Perigree Books, 1980), p. 154.
4 Sandra Stanley Holton, 'In Sorrowful Wrath: Suffrage Militancy and the Romantic Feminism of Emmeline Pankhurst', in Harold Smith (ed) *British Feminism in the Twentieth Century* (Edward Elgar, 1990), p. 9.
5 Brian Harrison, 'The Act of Militancy' in *Peaceable Kingdom, Stability and Change in Modern Britain* (Clarendon Press, 1982).
6 Ibid, p. 46.
7 T.D. Benson, *The Reformers' Year Book 1907* (Suffrage Collection, Museum of London).
8 L. Leneman, *'A Guid Cause': The Woman's Suffrage Movement in Scotland* (Aberdeen University Press, 1991).

9   Antonia Raeburn, *Militant Suffragettes* (New English Library, 1973), p. 206.
10   *The Times*, March 11th 1914.
11   George Dangerfield, *The Strange Death of Liberal England*, p. 155.
12   Christabel Pankhurst, Leaflet circa 1912.
13   *The Suffragette*, December 12th 1913.
14   Jane Marcus (ed), *Suffrage and the Pankhursts* (Routledge and Kegan Paul, 1987), p. 9.

Source-based questions on 'The Suffrage Campaigns'

1   The Suffragette Campaigns

Read the poem from Housman on page 50 and 'A Year's Record' on page 58.

a)   What is meant by 'Give us the vote that we may make the home a happier place' in Housman's poem (line 12)? (3 marks)

b)   List five different types of suffragette action given in 'A Year's Record'. (2 marks)

c)   How might a suffragette justify the destructive methods listed in 'A Year's Record'? (6 marks)

d)   To what extent does the poem help an historian understand the attitudes of suffrage supporters? (5 marks)

Summary Diagram
The Suffrage Campaigns

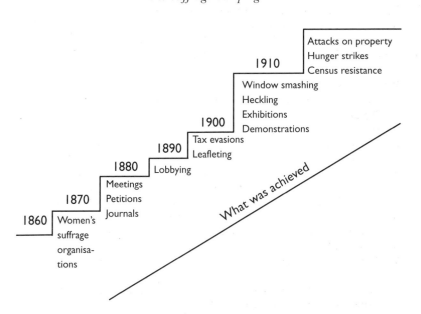

5 Men and Votes for Women

It is tempting to classify the struggle for votes for women as a battle of the sexes but, in fact, the lines of engagement between women and men were not so clearly drawn. At first, it appears that men generally disagreed with votes for women - certainly no government was prepared to enfranchise them. Indeed, mention of female suffrage within Parliament was often greeted by ribald laughter and antagonistic speeches. However, men, just like women, were not a homogeneous group but were made up of individuals from diverse economic and social backgrounds who held a variety of political views. As a consequence, there emerged several different male perspectives on women's suffrage. Undeniably, the response of men in general towards female suffrage was complex, and it is worth exploring the extent to which men either opposed or championed the suffrage movement. Despite setbacks, by 1914 suffrage had certainly become the foremost political question for women and was firmly on the national agenda of male politics.

1 The Political Parties

Even though suffrage eventually became headline news, no party before 1918 was prepared to adopt women's suffrage. As a result, all the suffrage bills in parliament were put forward by sympathetic MPs as private members' bills, which meant that they had little chance of success because they did not have majority party backing. Between 1860 and 1914 no bill for women's suffrage ever got beyond its second reading. (Each bill has to go through three readings in Parliament before it becomes law.) When women's suffrage was first debated, in 1867, there were 71 votes for and 123 against, but most abstained from voting. Practically every year for the following forty years a women's franchise bill was introduced - and failed. Eventually, in 1910, in an attempt to break the party deadlock, a group of MPs from all sides of the House of Commons formed a Conciliation Committee, which consisted of 25 Liberals, 17 Conservative, 6 Labour and 6 Irish Nationalists, to marshal support across party lines. This Committee continued the tradition of sponsoring private members bills but, although the MPs who presented each bill gained support from a few sympathisers, they faced greater opposition. Not only did each Bill fail but the debates surrounding them were sometimes facetious or hostile. In 1905 MPs debated for hours, with mock seriousness, a measure to compel carts on the road to carry rear lights - to avoid giving time to a bill on women's suffrage.

Why was women's suffrage so unsuccessful in gaining wholesale party approval? It has been argued that Conservatives disliked any extension of democracy, whereas the Liberals, fearful of the property-based qualification for the vote, were convinced that women would support the Conservatives. There was certainly a historical precedent for this fear because when the Liberals passed the Third Reform Bill in 1884 many of the agricultural labourers who were enfranchised voted Conservative. Labour, of course, much preferred universal franchise to what was perceived to be a middle-class female vote. However, such a clear-cut party interpretation underestimates the variety of opinions which existed within the parties concerned.

a) The Conservative Party

Votes for women found favour within some sections of the Conservative Party. Women's suffrage resolutions were passed at Conservative Party Annual Conferences in England on at least three occasions and by Scottish Annual Conferences more regularly. Most of the Conservative Party leadership seemed well-disposed towards votes for women: Prime Ministers Disraeli, Salisbury and Balfour, for example, all spoke in support. In 1866 Disraeli stated that 'I do not see ... on what reasons ... she has not a right to vote'[1], in 1888, Lord Salisbury believed 'that the day is not far distant when women will also bear their share in voting for members of Parliament and in determining the policy of the country'[2]; and in 1892 Balfour pointed out the contradiction in giving 'a vote to a man who contributes nothing to taxation but what he pays on his beer, while you refuse enfranchisement to a woman whatever her contribution to the state may be'.[3] Some Conservative MPs even promoted private members' bills within the House of Commons and worked hard for the all-party Conciliation Committee established in 1910.

However, as Rover suggests, there was no evidence of any great commitment by the Conservative leaders to implement women's suffrage when in office. When John Stuart Mill proposed a woman's suffrage amendment to the 1867 Reform Bill, Disraeli (who was prepared to take a 'leap in the dark' to extend the franchise to working-class men) offered no help towards its safe passage. Similarly Lord Salisbury did little to further the cause of women's suffrage and even voted against a second reading of a women's suffrage Bill in 1891. His nephew, Arthur Balfour, considered sympathetic to women's suffrage, again did little. When he was succeeded as Conservative leader by Bonar Law the suffrage movement fared no better: in 1913 Bonar Law declined to support an amendment to a franchise reform bill which would have enfranchised women.

The predominantly Conservative House of Lords was generally opposed to women's suffrage but there were notable exceptions. A few such as Lord Lytton, Constance Lytton's brother and President of the Men's League for Women's Suffrage, were in favour of Votes for Women and systematically promoted the cause within the House of Lords. However, most shared the views of Lord Curzon, who was antagonistic towards female suffrage. As Vice President of the Men's League for Opposing Women's Suffrage, he actively campaigned against votes for women. Curzon viewed suffrage militancy through the prism of misogyny, firmly believing that militancy resulted from the mental instability of women. Many Conservatives agreed with Curzon's sentiments and were convinced that madness would ensue once women were enfranchised. Rover, however, suggests that the reasons why women's suffrage never became a party issue was largely because of the generally antagonistic attitude of Conservative back-benchers towards any extension of the franchise rather than any particular aversion to women. Conservatives preferred to maintain the status quo and habitually objected to any measure of reform which might have increased democracy. Certainly, more Conservative backbenchers voted against women's suffrage than for it. Normally, even a reluctant Government would extend the vote if they thought the opposition, when in office, would do so. It was thought that whoever extended the vote was likely to gain the gratitude of those enfranchised and thus benefit from another term of office. However, the Liberals were unlikely to promote women's suffrage and so the Conservative leadership were not willing to endanger party unity over the issue.

b) The Liberal Party

While the Conservative leaders endorsed votes for women and the rank and file opposed it, the reverse was true of the Liberals. Most of the Liberal party membership agreed with women's suffrage, whereas the prime ministers tended to be opposed. The nineteenth century Prime Minister Gladstone disliked the idea of women's suffrage and let it be known that he, and any governments he formed, would resist any amendment to enfranchise women. When in office, Gladstone opposed a women's suffrage amendment to the 1884 Reform Bill on the grounds that it might endanger its successful passing. In a letter to an MP in 1892 he stated that 'The fear I have is, we should invite her unwittingly to trespass upon the delicacy, the purity, the refinement, the elevation of her own nature.'[4] In the early twentieth century Campbell-Bannerman privately expressed approval of votes for women but publicly blocked its progress in the House of Commons. Historians have pinpointed the entrenched position of Asquith, Prime Minister at the height of suffragette militancy, who obstructed any advance towards votes for women and persistently refused to see women's suffrage deputations. Asquith, although married to a very shrewd political operator, was unchanging in his implacable opposition to votes for women. In his first major speech on suffrage in 1892 Asquith gave four main reasons why he was against women's suffrage. Firstly he argued that the vast majority of women did not want the vote, secondly that women were not fit for the franchise, thirdly that women operated by personal influence, and finally that it would upset the natural order of things. Asquith believed that woman's place was in the home rather than in what he termed the 'dust and turmoil' of political life. Indeed Millicent Fawcett believed that it was Asquith more than any other person who prevented the Liberal Party from becoming the party to enfranchise women.

Although women's suffrage drew support from leading Liberal MPs, this support, as with the Conservatives, was fainthearted. Both Lloyd George and Winston Churchill advocated women's suffrage at various meetings but opposed the first Conciliation Bill of 1910 (see page 72) because it offered too limited a franchise. And, in 1912, when a further Conciliation Bill was being debated in Parliament, both Lloyd George and Winston Churchill were associated with a rumour that Asquith would resign if the Bill were passed. However, when he was Prime Minister, Lloyd George was responsible for the safe passage of the 1918 Reform Bill, which enfranchised women over the age of 30.

Despite the antagonism from prime ministers and the feeble support of leading Liberals, the women's suffrage movement received grass roots Liberal endorsement. A number of individual men gave generously of their time, money and energies to promote votes for women. The MP Jacob Bright, the philosopher John Stuart Mill, the barrister Richard Pankhurst and the philanthropist Frederick Pethwick Lawrence, were just some of many men who supported votes for women, often at the expense of other commitments. Between 1867 and 1886, when there were fifteen women's suffrage resolutions, the Liberals accounted for more than two thirds of the yes votes. And there is no doubt that the 25 Liberal MPs who worked hard for the Conciliation Committee were deeply committed to female suffrage.

c) The Labour Party

The Labour Party, which emerged from the Labour Representation Committee, was founded in the same year - 1906 - as the Liberals swept to power. Initially, the Labour Party's support for votes for women was somewhat muted as the Party was split over whether to champion women's suffrage at the expense of universal suffrage. Even in 1900, roughly 60 per cent of working-class men were excluded from the franchise as the right to vote was still based upon the owner-ship or occupation of property. Because women demanded the vote on the same terms as men, many Labour Party members (who saw universal suffrage as being of greater importance) were unsympa-thetic towards such an elitist measure. In addition it was feared that a limited franchise would be detrimental to the Labour Party as it would increase the political power of the propertied class and rein-force the class composition of the voting population. Indeed it became a socialist imperative to call for adult suffrage rather than female suffrage. Furthermore, by '1907 it had become more difficult to combine labour and suffrage politics'[5] particularly when the disruptive tactics of the suffragettes at by-elections strained any residual loyalties the labour movement held about votes for women.

A future leader of the Labour Party, Ramsey MacDonald, was certainly equivocal in his support of women's suffrage. Although MacDonald sympathised with women's suffrage and believed that it was a vital part of a socialist programme, he was not only overtly critical of the methods of the suffragettes but described them as silly children:

> 1   I have no objection to revolution, if it is necessary, but I have the very strongest objection to childishness masquerading as revolution, and all I can say of these window-breaking expeditions is that they are simply silly and provocative. I wish the working women of the
> 5   country who really care for the vote ... would come to London and tell these pettifogging middle-class damsels who are going out with little hammers in their muffs that if they do not go home they will get their heads broken.[6]

In contrast, three key Labour MPs, Keir Hardie, George Lansbury and Philip Snowden, took a more pragmatic view of reform. Men such as these argued that it was crucial to fight one step at a time and preferred to campaign for votes for women, which they claimed would affect the majority of working-class widows and spinsters, rather than wait for universal suffrage. Keir Hardie (a close friend of the Pankhursts, and one-time lover of Sylvia, who interestingly prophesied that universal suffrage would not be obtained until 1929) worked hard for women's suffrage both in and outside Parliament. Although he was often ridiculed in the House of Commons Keir Hardie's commitment never wavered. According to Sylvia Pankhurst, he collected funds, wrote leaflets, taught the suffragettes Parliamentary procedure, introduced them to influential people, visited them in prison and even condoned their violent tactics. Similarly Philip Snowden, MP and vice-president of the Men's League for Women's Suffrage, promoted WSPU policies at least until 1912 when suffragette militancy reached a new height. George Lansbury, MP for Bromley and Bow, also dedicated much of his political life to women's suffrage. He condoned suffragette violence, justifying it as a response to Government duplicity. On one occasion he rushed across the House of Commons floor, shook his fist at Asquith and shouted 'You'll go down to history as the man who tortured innocent women' in objection to the force-feeding of suffragettes. Moreover, Lansbury demanded that all Labour MPs vote against all Liberal Government proposals, even when they benefited the working class, until women were granted the vote. In 1912 he resigned his seat and sought re-election as an independent MP as a protest against the Labour Party's half-hearted commitment to women's suffrage. This was an act of great generosity - or foolishness - because Lansbury lost the election; indeed the social reformer, Beatrice Webb, wrote of him as having a great heart but little intellect.

Relationships between the Labour Party as a whole and the suffrage movement changed over time. At first the links between the two were strong, especially at a local level: after all, the Manchester-based WSPU was founded to improve the lives of working-class women. Certainly, the agitation for women's suffrage was seen to be inextricably bound up with labour politics. Many radical suffragists, not just the Pankhursts, joined the Labour Party. In 1906 the Women's Labour League was founded to provide socialist women with an organisational base from which to raise the issue of votes for women within the labour movement. Local Labour groups often supported women's suffrage: the Woolwich Labour Party, for example, consistently supported the aims and methods of the WSPU because they realised that even a limited extension of the franchise would enfranchise a respectable number of working-class widows and spinsters. However, not all local groups supported the suffrage movement. Lewisham Borough Council for instance laughingly declined to support women's suffrage when a motion was being debated at a Council meeting. Moreover, the friendly relationship which existed between the WSPU and the Labour Party soured when the former engaged in violent behaviour and the latter refused to join George Lansbury in his opposition to the Liberal Government.

Gradually, as the mutual antagonism between the suffrage movement and the Labour Party receded, those in favour of votes for women won the day. From 1910 onwards all Labour MPs voted in support of women's suffrage and from 1912 the NUWSS and the Labour Party formed an electoral alliance. Eventually in 1912 the Labour Party became the first major political party to include votes for women in their manifesto. Nevertheless, support for female suffrage from such a minority party (the Labour Party only had 42 MPs at the time) did not guarantee success in Parliament.

2 The Liberal Government 1906-14

a) Reaction to Peaceful Campaigning

From 1906, when the Liberals were in office, votes for women depended on them to promote or give time to bills on women's suffrage. The Liberal Government enjoyed a large majority in 1906 and therefore had the Parliamentary power to enfranchise women. Historians have suggested that the Liberals were reluctant to do so for three main reasons. Firstly, the Prime Minister, Asquith, was hostile to votes for women. Secondly, its majority was gradually whittled down by a series of elections and from 1910 it relied on the votes from the Irish Nationalists and the Labour Party to stay in office. It was unwilling to jeopardise its term of government (the Irish Nationalists were not in favour of giving Parliamentary time to women's suffrage) for the sake of votes for women. Thirdly, the Liberals had other, more pressing, problems with which to grapple. They faced insurrection in Ireland, rebellion by the House of Lords and widespread strike action by trade unionists: a period characterised by George Dangerfield as revolutionary. This cataclysmic state of affairs perhaps explains the unwillingness of a Liberal government to put time aside for a women's suffrage bill.

However, these suggestions can be considered excuses rather than explanations. As we have seen previously, the Liberals were ambivalent about women's suffrage and refused to promote it. Constantly, and with consummate skill, the government undercut the efforts of the advocates of women's suffrage. The following catalogue of failed bills tends to support this argument:

The Liberal Government and Votes for Women

1906 Government refused to support an amendment to a Plural Voting Bill which would have enfranchised a number of propertied women.
1907 Women's Suffrage Bill rejected.
1908 Women's Suffrage Bill carried.
1909 Second Reading of Women's Suffrage Bill carried but Asquith failed to give support so the Bill failed.
1910 First Conciliation Bill carried but ultimately failed because the Government refused to grant it Parliamentary time.
1911 Second Conciliation Bill carried but Asquith announced that he preferred to support manhood suffrage but which could include an amendment for the enfranchisement of women.
1913 Government Franchise Bill introduced universal male suffrage but an amendment to enfranchise women was declared unconstitutional.

Time after time, women were led to believe that votes for women were achievable only to be humiliated by what was perceived to be a duplicitous government. Ultimately, of course, the Liberal Government was considered by the suffragettes not just equivocal in its response to votes for women but antagonistic. The response of the Liberal Government towards women who broke the law certainly suggests that it was hostile to votes for women. There was a decided contrast between the treatment meted out to the law-breaking Ulster Unionists (who preached sedition in Belfast and smuggled guns to help a rebellion against the forthcoming partition of Ireland), and the law-breaking suffragettes. A blind eye was turned to the gun smuggling of the Ulster rebels who remained immune from arrest and were consulted over Ireland, whereas the suffragettes were first ignored and then harassed, arrested, imprisoned, and force-fed.

When the Women's Social and Political Union (WSPU) began its illegal activities, the Liberal government reacted by denying them democratic forms of protest. In an attempt to stop potential disruption, women were forbidden to attend Liberal meetings unless they held a signed ticket. The Government refused to meet deputations or accept petitions, banned meetings in public places and censored the press in an attempt to silence the WSPU. The Commissioner of Police, directed by the Home Office, refused to allow suffragettes to hold meetings in any London parks and persuaded the management at the Albert Hall not to let it out to suffragettes. When the WSPU managed to hire a different venue, the owner of the hall was threatened with the withdrawal of his licence. The Government also prosecuted the printer who printed *The Suffragette*, periodically raided the offices and homes of the WSPU members and eventually forced Christabel Pankhurst to flee to Paris, where she directed the movement from exile.

On numerous occasions the Government acted even more harshly towards the suffragettes. As Home Secretary in charge of civil order, Winston Churchill was held responsible for the notorious police violence towards women on Friday November 18th 1910, later termed 'Black Friday' by the suffragettes. On this day approximately three hundred suffragettes marched to the House of Commons in protest at the failure of the first Conciliation Bill. When they tried to enter Parliament the police behaved with unexpected brutality. The police, instructed not to arrest the suffragettes, forced the women back, kicked them, twisted their breasts, punched their noses and thrust knees between their legs. All the 135 statements made by the suffragettes testify to the violence: 'I was seized by several policemen. One twisted my right arm behind my back with such brutal force, that I really thought he would break it ... Another policemen gave me a terrible blow in my back, which sent me whirling among the crowd'[7], said one 60-year-old woman, and 29 women testified to some form of sexual assault.

Historians offer different interpretations of this event. Rosen excuses police cruelty by suggesting that the force brought in for this day were too inexperienced in handling suffragette demonstrations. In the past, he argues, they had been used to policing the rough and tough working class of the East End rather than young, genteel, middle-class women, and so were at a loss as to what the correct procedure might be. In addition, women, by their very femininity, were seen to provoke police violence. 'By attempting to rush through or past police lines, these women were bringing themselves repeatedly into abrupt physical contact with the police. That the police found in the youthful femininity of many of their assailants an invitation to licence, does not seem, all in all, completely surprising'[8]. In contrast, Susan Kingsley Kent and Martha Vicinus argue that the violence directed at the suffragettes was in fact sexual abuse. The cruelty meted out by the police is seen by such historians to be a direct result of the domestic ideology of Victorian and Edwardian Britain, whereby respectable women remained in the private sphere of home while only men and prostitutes entered the public sphere of the streets. Hence, when suffragettes demonstrated outside the male Parliament they were perceived to be no better than prostitutes. Because of this, and in order to protect their public space, men were willing to permit, even encourage, 'the violation of woman's most intimate space - her body'.[9]

b) Reaction to Violent Campaigning

The Liberal Government also imprisoned suffragettes who broke the law. At first women, given 'First Division' treatment, were awarded the status of political prisoners, and so allowed to wear their own clothes and receive food parcels. After 1908, however, women were placed in the 'Second Division', being regarded as criminals rather than political dissidents and having the privileges they had once enjoyed taken away. From this time on they were treated just like ordinary prisoners. Until the work of June Purvis[10], the prison treatment of women has been neglected by historians. She argues that the prison authorities hoped to undermine suffragettes by making them endure ritualistic humiliation which took away their sense of self. Prisoners had to remain silent, were locked in separate cells, forced to wear prison clothes and were referred to by their prison number rather than their name. Daily life was well regulated and equally demeaning. Prisoners were woken at 5:30 a.m., ate a breakfast of tea, brown bread and butter; at 7 a.m. they had to empty the slops, scrub the cell floor and clean their tin utensils and fold their bedclothes. Baths were taken weekly and books borrowed twice a week. Each prisoner was expected to do prison work such as making night-gowns or knitting socks. At 8 p.m. the cell light was switched off. Contact with the outside world was limited - and censored. All correspondence was read by the prison authorities which once more served to humiliate the suffragette prisoner because it invaded her privacy.

When women responded to their imprisonment by hunger-striking the Home Secretary, Reginald McKenna, in a debate in the House of Commons on June 11th 1914, suggested four solutions to this problem:

1 So far as I am aware these are four, and four only in number. I have had unlimited correspondence from every section of the public who have been good enough to advise me as to what I ought to do, and among them all I have not been able to discover more than four
5 alternative methods. The first, is to let them die. That is, I should say, at the present moment, the most popular, judging by the number of

letters I have received. The second is to deport them. The third is to treat them as lunatic, and the fourth is to give them the franchise ... I think we should not adopt any of them.

At first, hunger strikers were released from prison but soon the government introduced force-feeding for women who consistently refused to eat. Once again, historians are divided over the significance of this course of action. Some historians justify the force-feeding of suffragettes because it saved the lives of those on hunger strike. Roger Fulford dismisses the force-feeding by the Liberal Government as a harmless procedure which had been in use for years with 'lunatics'. Early feminist historians tended to agree with these interpretations. In particular, socialist feminist historians, often antagonistic to the suffragettes, underplay the brutality of the government towards women. In stark contrast, much of the pictorial propaganda of the suffragettes represented force-feeding as oral rape. Later feminist historians subscribed to this image, arguing that the 'instrumental invasion of the body, accompanied by overpowering physical force, great suffering and humiliation was akin to it'.[11] Over a thousand women endured what Marcus calls the public violation of their bodies as they were force-fed through the nostril, the mouth and even the rectum and vagina. Sometimes the tubes used were not sterile and had been used before which increased the sense of outrage of those who had been force-fed. On August 12th 1912, the medical journal *The Lancet*, outraged by forcible feeding, described it as follows

1 Prisoners were held down by force, flung on the floor, tied to chairs and iron bedsteads ... while the tube was forced up the nostrils. After each feeding the nasal pain gets worse. The wardress endeavoured to make the prisoner open her mouth by sawing the edge of
5 the cup along the gums... the broken edge caused laceration and severe pain. Food into the lung of one unresisting prisoner immediately caused severe choking, vomiting ... persistent coughing. She was hurriedly released next day suffering from pneumonia and pleurisy. We cannot believe that any of our colleagues will agree that this form
10 of prison treatment is justly described in Mr McKenna's words as necessary medical treatment.

Force-feeding, and the association of hunger strikers with lunatics, certainly seems to suggest that the Government was deeply hostile to suffragette prisoners, but it could equally suggest that the Liberal Government chose this method because it was alarmed at the prospect of women dying in prison. Nonetheless, the Government chose its victims with care. On the one hand, influential women like Lady Constance Lytton and Mrs Brailsford (wife of an important journalist who supported the Liberal party) were released from prison when they went on hunger strike, whereas working-class women, received quite different treatment (see page 59).

On April 25th 1913, as a result of adverse publicity, the Prisoners' Temporary Discharge for Ill-Health Act became law. This temporarily released persistent hunger strikers from prison to give them time to recover. As soon as they were better they were required to return to prison. Not surprisingly, no woman went back to prison voluntarily. Consequently the police kept released prisoners under surveillance, arrested them and imprisoned them without trial for the same offence once they were deemed to be fit enough to serve their sentence. This new piece of legislation may have been an ingenious device by the Government to put an end to hunger striking but it was soon dubbed mockingly the 'Cat and Mouse Act' by the suffragettes, as shown by the propaganda poster on page 77.

Of course, it could be argued that the Liberal Government were merely responding in a rational way to an increasing level of suffragette violence. To enfranchise women under such circumstance might well set a dangerous precedent: future protest groups could be tempted to use similar methods to achieve their goal.

3 The Alternative Establishment

The male 'alternative establishment', that is the trade unions, religious groups and the press, was as divided as the political parties over the question of votes for women. Although the leadership of the majority of trade unions seemed to be indifferent to women's suffrage, a number of them supported it. Similarly, whereas the official Church was unresponsive to votes for women, some committed individual clergy campaigned vigorously for the cause. The press, depending on its political allegiances, also responded in a variety of ways. However, there is still a lot of research needed in these areas and so it is impossible to reach any firm conclusion.

a) Trade Unions

The trade union movement as a whole was split over the question of votes for women. John Burns, a notable trade unionist, was implacably opposed to women's suffrage, whereas others agreed with it. According to Liddington and Norris, the official union response ranged from 'benign indifference to downright hostility'.[12] Although the Trades Union Congress (TUC) had passed a resolution in 1884 in favour of votes for women, little had been done to promote women's suffrage in practice. What is more, when the issue was raised 17 years later at another TUC Conference (where there were only four women delegates), it drew an antagonistic rather than a supportive response. Indeed, the National Union of Miners (NUM), which controlled a large block of votes, opposed a resolution on women's suffrage at the 1912 Labour Party Conference.

However, not all the trade union movement was antagonistic as, like

Propaganda poster produced by the WSPU

the Labour Party, it responded differently at individual and local levels. For example, one of the miners' leaders, Robert Smillie, advocated strike action in support of women's suffrage, and a member of the National Transport Workers' Federation was arrested and imprisoned for two months for breaking windows as a protest against the unjust imprisonment of suffragettes. In Lancashire, a textile area with a history of women's active participation in the trade union movement, several weavers' unions sent petitions to Parliament and encouraged Labour MPs to introduce women's suffrage into the House of Commons. In the East End of London, Sylvia Pankhurst's East London Federation of Suffragettes (ELFS) drew support from large sections of the male working class - dockers, seamen, gas workers, labourers, firemen and post office workers - many of whom came on demonstrations and protected the ELFS members from gangs of unruly local youths. Indeed, one prize-fighter from the East End became Sylvia Pankhurst's personal bodyguard. Glasgow dockers also supported the WSPU.

b) Religious Groups

Historians have virtually ignored the response of official religion to women's suffrage, even though religion played a significant role in people's lives in the nineteenth and early twentieth centuries. Despite this lack of research, it seems safe to say that religious groups responded to women's suffrage in diverse ways. The Church of England was somewhat ambivalent, whereas nonconformists, (Protestants outside the Church of England) and Quakers, in particular, sometimes gave unqualified support. To date, there has been no published research on either the Roman Catholic or Judaism's response though it is known that a Canon of a Roman Catholic Church in London supported votes for women suffrage, as did the Chief Rabbi. Catholic congregations seemed less enthusiastic than their clergy, if the experience of the ELFS was common: when a group tried to pray for women's suffrage in a Roman Catholic Church in Poplar they were beaten up by the people attending.

Throughout this period the Church of England maintained a discreet silence over the question of women's suffrage and was later criticised by the suffragettes for doing so. The WSPU condemned the church for being 'shamefully and obsequiously compliant' and for being 'degraded into the position of hanger-on and lackey of the Government'.[13] The Church of England, acting through the Bishops in the House of Lords, was also censured for helping the Government to pass the Cat and Mouse Act. Indeed the Church of England was thought to disapprove more of militancy than forcible feeding, and this prompted the WSPU to indict the Church:

1   with having aided and abetted the State in robbing women of the
    vote. The Church is thus held guilty of the subjection of women and
    all the vice, suffering and social degradation that result from that
    subjection. Whereas it is the duty of the Church to insist upon the
5   political enfranchisement of women - not only as a political reform,
    but as a moral and even a religious reform - the Church has actually
    boycotted this great question and has condoned the torture of the
    women who are fighting for their liberty.[14]

Nevertheless a number of individual clergy responded positively to women's suffrage. Some significant leaders of Anglican religious thought in the early twentieth century - the Archbishop of Canterbury, the Lord Bishop of Exeter, the Lord Bishop of Hereford, the Lord Bishop of Liverpool and the Right Rev. Bishop of Edinburgh - favoured votes for women. A number of clergy, who argued that women's suffrage harmonised with essential Christian principles of equality, established a Church League for Women's Suffrage to promote the cause. The Rector of Whitburn, for example, said that the:

1   extension of the Suffrage to women seems to me a logical sequence
    of Christian principle. In the Christian society there is no superior
    sex, the equality of each member is recognised, the individuality of
    each person is sacred. St Paul asserted this when he wrote: 'in
5   baptism there is neither male nor female'. The rights of each are
    equal, therefore women are entitled to express their convictions and
    assert their individuality by voting if they choose to do so.[15]

Similarly, the Vicar at Kirkby Lonsdale believed that because Jesus Christ encouraged a certain freedom and independence in the conduct of women then it followed that Christians should support women's suffrage. Others believed women to be the moral guardians of the nation and the family who, once enfranchised, would exercise a beneficial influence on these areas. And when forcible feeding was introduced, a large number of these clergy protested against it.

The connections between suffrage and nonconformism appear much stronger. This may have been because nonconformist women, unlike those in the Church of England, played a leading role. For example, the Labour Churches, founded in Manchester in the latter part of the nineteenth century, encouraged women to participate on equal terms and invited suffragettes like Hannah Mitchell to speak to their congregations on votes for women. Similarly, the Quakers, were sympathetic to women's suffrage. Quaker women enjoyed equal rights with male Quakers, having the opportunity both to speak at religious meetings and to participate in political activity. Quakers were especially motivated by a sense of moral purpose and took a leading role in many reform movements such as anti-slavery, education for women and opposition to the Contagious Diseases Acts (CDAs).

c) The Press

Until the work by Laura Ogilini, the press, just as religion, had been largely ignored by suffrage scholars, but there are a few general points one can make. Before the illegal activities of the WSPU provided headline-catching news, most newspapers disregarded the women's suffrage movement. After 1905, when Christabel Pankhurst and Annie Kenney were arrested, newspapers took more notice of suffragette activity. However, the press often reported militancy in ways which were condemnatory rather than complimentary or neutral. Once the militant campaign escalated, the response to the suffragettes grew even more hostile, with the press describing the suffragettes as mad, bad and dangerous to know. *The Times*, in particular, was most unsympathetic. In 1912 it viewed the suffragettes as 'regrettable bye-products of our civilisation, out with their hammers and their bags full of stones because of dreary, empty lives and high-strung, over-excitable natures'.[16] Letters to *The Times* also suggest a deep antagonism towards women's suffrage, especially when comparisons were drawn between suffragette militancy and 'the explosive fury of epileptics'.[17] In a similar fashion the *London Standard* condemned militancy as the act of deranged lunatics and a 'form of hysteria of a highly dangerous type'.[18] Both the *Daily Mirror* and the *Illustrated London News* carried full pages of photographs of suffragettes being assaulted on Black Friday which, because of their sexually suggestive nature, were guaranteed to appeal to the voyeuristic.

Not all newspapers were unsympathetic. At the other end of the political spectrum, *The Workman's Times* supported votes for women. Nevertheless, it shared more than a name in common with the 'official' *Times* as it too believed that women's place was in the home not the workplace.[19] Some men even published their own newspapers in support of votes for women: in 1907 J Francis began a weekly paper, *Women's Franchise*. Some local newspapers also gave qualified approval to votes for women: the *Lewisham Borough News*, for example, was sympathetic to women's suffrage but criticised the militant tactics of the WSPU.[20]

4 Male Organisations

Men could be members of the NUWSS but were not eligible to join the WSPU because the suffrage struggle was seen as a women's movement which could only be conducted by women. Thus, men founded their own organisations to support the suffragettes: the Men's League for Women's Suffrage and the Men's Federation for Women's Suffrage, which later became the Men's Political Union, were two of the most important. There were also local men's organisations such as the Rebels Social and Political Union and the East London Men's

Society in the East End of London, and the Northern Men's
Federation for Women's Suffrage in the north of Britain.

The first male-only organisation, the Men's League for Women's
Suffrage, was established in 1907 and numbered amongst its members
men from all shades of political opinion. Any man, whatever his political or religious persuasion, was welcome to join. It formed branches
all over Britain: a branch was even formed as far north as Inverness.
Although the League was founded by Emmeline Pethwick Lawrence's
brother-in-law and had Lord Lytton as President, it appeared to have
more in common with the NUWSS and the WFL - both Fawcett and
Despard (notably not the Pankhursts) attended its first public
meeting - rather than the WSPU. Furthermore, the League favoured
the law-abiding, peaceful methods of the NUWSS, rather than the law-
breaking confrontational style of the WSPU as the leaflet advertising
their first public meeting in 1907 demonstrates:

1 We do not proceed by any uproarious methods; we content
   ourselves with appealing to the thoughtfulness of men, ... in this very
   slow moving country of ours no great movement can be carried
   through unless it is accompanied by what people at the time very
5 likely think to be outrageous conduct ... we can do without it,
   because what we have to do is to show to the men voters in this
   country that the claim, the demand, the women are making is ... a
   claim which politically expediency ought to be only too ready to
   extend.[21]

Members of the League participated in demonstrations, wrote leaflets
and pamphlets, organised petitions, lobbied MPs in support of
women's suffrage and acted as a conduit between the suffragists and
the government.

The second major organisation, the Men's Federation for Women's
Suffrage, which was later renamed the Men's Political Union, was
formally constituted in 1910. The Federation drew upon a more
radical tradition than the League:

1 Firstly, the policy of this Union is action, entirely independent of
   political parties; secondly opposition to whatever government is in
   power, until such time as the franchise is granted; thirdly, participation in parliamentary elections in opposition to the government
5 candidate, and independently of all other candidates; and lastly,
   vigorous agitation and the education of public opinion by all the usual
   methods, such as public meetings, demonstrations, debates, distribution of literature, newspaper correspondence and deputations to
   public representatives.

The Federation identified more with the WSPU, using the same
suffragette colours of purple, white and green, than with the NUWSS.
It believed that if men were really anxious to help women achieve the
vote they should sever all connections with party politics and devote

their energies to the suffrage cause. There is no doubt that many men who belonged to the Federation gave much time and commitment to women's suffrage, combining traditional forms of protest with militant ones. The Federation helped organise demonstrations: for instance it supported a Trafalgar Square demonstration from the East End of London for the ELFS. When women were shut out of Liberal meetings, members of the Federation went in to represent them. It also heckled Liberal ministers: one man had his leg fractured in two places when he was thrown out of a meeting of Churchill's in Bradford. Another man attacked Winston Churchill with a whip; two more threw mouse traps at the MPs in Parliament from the Strangers Gallery in protest at the Cat and Mouse Act; others broke windows; yet others attempted arson - Harold Laski, for example, tried to destroy a railway station in 1913. As a result of these protests, men were imprisoned, and like women, went on hunger strike and were either released under the Cat and Mouse Act or else forcibly fed. One man who had set fire to a railway carriage, was convicted, imprisoned and force-fed 114 times when he refused to eat.

The WSPU initially welcomed this kind of male support, but by 1912 the Federation found itself out of favour with the WSPU. Indeed Emmeline Pethick Lawrence stated that 'Men in prison only embarrass us.' As Sandra Holton points out, male violence was different from women's.[22] Firstly, she argues, female violence could be justified because women were excluded from traditional peaceful forms of political protest: because they had the vote, men could make their voices heard within the constitution, without recourse to violence. Hence, Holton argues, male violence was seen by the WSPU to 'threaten the legitimacy of militant protest'. Secondly, suffragette militancy was justified by the suffragettes as part of a sex war with heroic, freedom-fighting women pitted against intransigent and violent men. The men who fought so hard for women's suffrage undermined this particular narrative because, as men, they were the enemy but, as members of the Federation, they were friends. Nevertheless, although exact figures are unknown, the number of men who joined the Federation was minuscule, allowing the suffragettes to maintain their beliefs about men in general.

As Brian Harrison points out, men also formed organisations to oppose women's suffrage. In 1909 a Men's League for Opposing Women's Suffrage was formed. It used similar tactics to the suffragists: they campaigned across the country, held meetings, collected signatures, and raised funds. In some respects it did rather better than its opponents. During 1908 it collected 337,018 signatures against votes for women, whereas the suffragists only managed to obtain 288,736 a year later. Nevertheless, membership of this group remained small, amounting to only 9,000.

5 Conclusion

The suffrage movement may have received a mixed response from those men who belonged to formal organisations, but it seemed unsuccessful in convincing the majority of British men. The evidence that is available - from famous individuals; from popular music hall songs; from the banning of women from certain places; and from the increasing level of violence in the crowds that gathered around women's demonstrations - points to a generally hostile response. However, it is difficult - if not impossible - to measure the extent to which these particular groups were representative of male opinion as a whole. In addition, research on the history of men and the suffrage movement remains sparse, making it hard to assess the level of either sympathy or hostility from men in general. It is tempting to suppose that the majority of men were apathetic and impartial rather than antagonistic but the evidence so far suggests that historians cannot make any very definite worthwhile judgements either way.

Historians claim that many aristocratic and upper-class men were opposed to votes for women. One famous doctor remarked in 1912 that 'there is mixed up with the women's movement much mental disorder'. London's male clubland generally opposed female suffrage, as did the Oxford Union. The royal family also opposed female suffrage: Edward VII was quite definitely against giving the vote to women. However, once again, these are just impressions based on a few individual comments and cannot be taken as representative of a whole social class.

Popular culture, in the form of Music hall songs and cartoons, offer entertaining insights into the minds of some men. The following popular song suggests that public opinion was negative but how many men listened to it is unknown.

> Put me upon an island where the girls are few
> Put me among the most ferocious lions in the zoo
> Put me in a prison and I'll never never fret
> But for pity's sake don't put me near a suffering-gette

The citadels of high culture certainly appeared unsympathetic to women's suffrage. Fear of militancy closed many of the country's art galleries and museums to the public completely or sometimes to women only. The rule of 'No muffs, wrist bags or sticks' was wide-spread: the Royal Academy and the Tate Gallery were closed to women and the British Museum announced that it was open to all men but only open to women if accompanied by men who were willing to vouch for their good behaviour. Unaccompanied women they said 'were only allowed in on presentation of a letter of introduction from a responsible person vouching for the bearer's good behaviour and accepting responsibility for her acts'. Again, this response may be evidence of justifiable anxiety about the prospect of suffragette violence rather than of an unfriendly attitude.

Recent research indicates that many suffragettes were violently and indecently assaulted when they participated in demonstrations. The occasions on which women had to put up with violent sexual harassment were numerous: they were often intimidated, harassed, and the victims of anti-suffrage rioting. Antagonistic men often sexually harassed women on demonstrations, ripping their clothes and whispering obscenities in their ears. Rosen has told of the number of men who came expressly to suffragette demonstrations to bully and sexually abuse women. Gangs of 'roughs' lay in wait for suffragettes who tried to get into the House of Commons. In Glasgow in March 1912, 200 men broke up the WSPU shop by throwing iron bolts and weights through the windows. At the Eisteddfod in Wales that year suffragettes who dared to heckle the local hero Lloyd George were seriously assaulted, their hair pulled and their clothing ripped - one woman was stripped to the waist, two women's shirts were cut up and the pieces given to the crowd. At another time the Croydon branch of the WSPU window was smashed and a WSPU stall in Walsall wrecked. Time and time again the suffragettes were subjected to brutal and sometimes sexual harassment so that it became impossible for the WSPU to hold outdoor meetings because they feared violence by the crowd gathered to watch. If this considerable, indiscriminate hostility is indicative of men's response then it seems as if they were vehemently opposed to women's suffrage. However, men who assaulted women were still very much in the minority so this type of harassment should not be taken as an indication of widespread male hostility.

Suffragists and suffragettes may have received an antagonistic response from some men but they drew support from unexpected quarters. Diane Atkinson has noted that many leading department stores, both in London and the provinces, displayed the WSPU colours in their windows. In 1908 in Lewisham, one large department store employed a WSPU speaker to address one of their sports day events while Sainsburys' exhibited clothes of green purple and white in their windows. Many other retail stores stocked clothes and other items in the suffragette colours. In 1910 the Votes for Women slogan was even printed on the wrappers of Allison's bread. This, of course, may have been just good business sense - the suffragettes were seen to be wealthy customers - but the displaying of suffragette colours may have antagonised more people than it attracted.

There is still much more research needed on men and the women's suffrage movement but the history written so far has been affected by distinct social trends. At first, women's suffrage was subsumed under men's history: for example, George Dangerfield's book examined the suffrage movement as part of a general Liberal political decline. With the rise of a separate women's history in the 1970s, women's suffrage became part of that history with the result that the wider political debate was ignored. In a curious twist of historiography, suffrage history came to be built around the ultimately victorious female with men largely eliminated from the story except as the enemy to be overcome. Just as women used to be hidden from men's history, so men today are hidden from women's suffrage history. Until 1997 when *The Men's Sphere* was published there had virtually been no research on organised male support of suffrage, of the responses of religious organisations or of newspaper coverage. Of course, histories which exclude these topics - like histories which exclude women - are not only inadequate but inaccurate because they portray only a partial view of of the world. Historians must therefore question the *female* bias in suffrage history, *men's* invisibility, and argue for a reappraisal of history based on the experiences of both sexes.

Nonetheless, it is odd to write about men's involvement in what was essentially a women's movement. Men's support of the suffrage campaign certainly raises important questions about the traditional role of men and women. Men who supported the female franchise usually acted in a supportive capacity to women. This of course is an interesting reversal of usual practice as it is usually women who take a back seat in political movements. What is more, even the men who opposed women's suffrage reacted to events rather than initiated them, a role reversal which, paradoxically, must have ultimately undermined their beliefs about women's role in society.

By the outbreak of war in 1914 the suffrage movement had reached an impasse. Although there were considerable numbers of men, across the class, political and religious spectrum, who supported women's suffrage, there were also considerable numbers who opposed it. Nevertheless, there was still a clear trend towards greater acceptance of the female vote. Parliament appeared little different from the nation at large in that MPs held a variety of opinions towards women's suffrage, ranging from sympathetic and indifferent to hostile. Liberal commitment to votes for women was muted, largely because of the intransigence of Asquith; Conservative opinion was generally opposed; while Labour was too insignificant a party to have much effect at all. It would take the trauma of war to break this particular deadlock.

References

1   *Leaflet of Conservative and Unionist Women's Franchise Association,* April 27th, 1866.
2   *Leaflet of Conservative and Unionist Women's Franchise Association,* November 12th, 1888.
3   *Leaflet of Conservative and Unionist Women's Franchise Association,* April 27th, 1892.
4   Constance Rover, *Women's Suffrage and Party Politics in Britain, 1866-1914* (Routledge and Kegan Paul, 1967), p. 120.
5   June Hannam 'In the Comradeship of the Sexes Lies the Hope of Progress and Social Regeneration: Women in the West Riding ILP,

c.1890-1914' in J. Rendal (ed), *Equal or Different*, (Basil Blackwell, 1987), p. 230.

6   David Marquand, *Ramsay MacDonald* (Jonathan Cape, 1977), p.148.

7   Mrs Matilda Mullins, (No 25) aged 60, Suffragette Testimonies from Museum of London Suffragette Collection.

8   A. Rosen, *Rise Up Women: The Militant Campaign of the WSPU 1903-1914* (Routledge and Kegan Paul, 1974), p. 145.

9   Martha Vicinus, *Independent Women* (Routledge, 1985), p. 261.

10 June Purvis 'The Prison Experiences of the Suffragettes in Edwardian Britain', *Women's History Review*, Vol 4 No 1 1995.

11 June Purvis 'The Prison Experiences of the Suffragettes in Edwardian Britain'.

12 Liddington and Norris, *One Hand Tied Behind Us* (Virago, 1978) p. 150.

13 Leaflet printed by the WSPU c. 1912.

14 WSPU *Annual Report*, 1914.

15 *Opinions of Leaders of Religious Thought* (Central Society for Women's Suffrage, 1905), p. 10.

16 Brian Harrison, *Separate Spheres: The Opposition to Women's Suffrage in Britain* (Croom Helm, 1978,) p. 33.

17 Ibid, p. 28.

18 Ibid, p. 28.

19 Laura Ogilini, in Angela John and Clare Eustance, *The Men's Share* (Routledge, 1997), p. 73.

20 Iris Dove, *Yours in the Cause* (Lewisham Library Service and Greenwich Library, 1988), p. 10.

21 Leaflet of Men's League for Women's Suffrage, December 1907.

22 Sandra Stanley Holton in *The Men's Share*, p. 15.

Source-based questions on 'Men and Votes for Women'

1. Men and votes for women

Read the extracts from the League for Women's Suffrage and the Men's Federation on page 81 and look at the poster on page 77.

a) Explain what is meant by 'uproarious methods' (line 1). (2 marks)

b) What seem to be the main differences between these two organisations, as expressed in these two extracts? (5 marks)

c) Look at the poster of the Cat and Mouse Act. Why was it called this? (2 marks)

d) Explain the significance of this poster as a piece of propaganda. (4 marks)

Summary Diagram
Men and Votes for Women

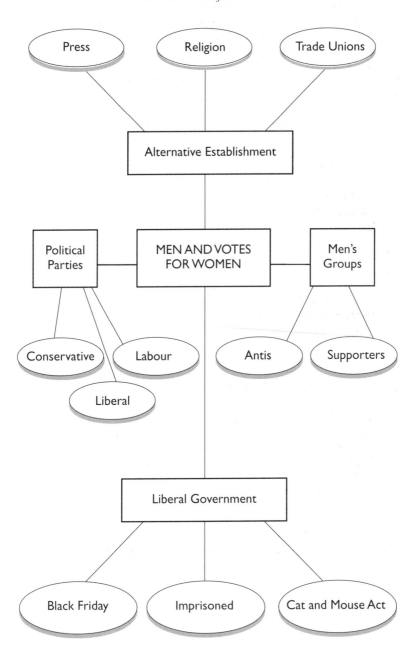

6 Women, Suffrage and the First World War

The First World War had a profound effect on suffrage politics. In August 1914, as Britain was going to war against Germany, the WSPU declared peace with the Liberals - the sex war, as Martin Pugh has pointed out, was swamped by the Great War. In one of her characteristic aphorisms, Emmeline Pankhurst remarked that there was no point in continuing to fight for the vote when there might be no country to vote in. The rest of the major suffrage societies agreed with her, discontinued their suffrage campaign and shifted their energies to the war effort.

However, it has been argued that the greatest effect of the war on women's suffrage was that women were granted the vote towards the end of it. On February 6th 1918, eight million women, out of an electorate of twenty-one million, were given the opportunity to vote. Until fairly recently, historians generally agreed that women were awarded the vote as a token of gratitude for their war work. 'The highly skilled and dangerous work done by women during the war in the armament and munitions factories and in auxiliary and nursing service at the Front was probably the greatest factor in the granting of the vote to women at the end of the war.'[1] However, the evidence for this interpretation is inconclusive and several historians have questioned the direct correlation between women's war work and women's suffrage. They argue that the emphasis placed on women's economic contribution to the war discounts the groundwork put in by the pre-war suffrage campaign. To complicate matters, a few historians have even suggested that the war, far from facilitating votes for women, actually postponed its implementation. Women's suffrage, they suggest, was on the verge of being granted just before the war broke out. This chapter will explore these controversies, examine the responses of the suffrage movement towards the war and consider the reasons for the success of women's suffrage in 1918.

1 The Suffrage Movement and the War

It may seem reasonable to suppose that the mature response of both the suffragettes and the suffragists in leading their organisations to support the war effort helped women gain the vote. Yet, while this is a plausible explanation, it is only partially valid as the response of the women's suffrage movement to war was varied. What is noticeable in the histories of the suffrage movement during the war is that although the WSPU led the way in patriotism, followed less enthusiastically by the NUWSS, others were reluctant to support what was perceived as an imperialist war. Nonetheless it is safe to say that, at the least, war overshadowed suffrage activities.

a) The Women's Social and Political Union

When war was declared in August 1914 the WSPU suspended suffrage activities and called upon its members to support the war effort. War raised the emotional intensity of the leadership to a new xenophobic level as both Christabel and Emmeline Pankhurst adopted an extremely nationalistic position. Both mother and daughter succumbed to British propaganda and saw the war, just as they had the suffrage question, in very simplistic terms with the 'goodies' fighting the 'baddies'. The Pankhursts viewed the war as a battle between the enlightened democracy of Britain and the autocratic militarism of Wilhelmine Germany. Germany - like their previous enemy the Liberal Government - was depicted as the world's bully who overrode every principle of humanity and morality and whose unbridled aggression had most certainly caused the war. At a meeting held at the London Opera House in September 1914, Christabel Pankhurst extolled the virtues of living under the British system and pleaded for Britain to support the 'feminine' state of France which had been threatened by the 'over-masculine state' of Germany.[2] God, according to the Pankhursts, was firmly on the British side.

The outbreak of war enabled the WSPU and its members to abandon their violent methods, demonstrate their patriotic loyalty and ultimately their deservedness of the vote. (Unsympathetic observers also claimed that the war accorded perfectly with their militaristic tendencies!) Within a few days of war, Emily Pankhurst threw herself into a vigorous campaign in which the defeat of Germany took priority over women's suffrage. And with somewhat alarming alacrity, the WSPU placed its organisation, and its funds, at the disposal of the Government, which by 1915 was desperate to recruit women workers. From 1915 onwards there was a great shortage of labour: two million men had joined the armed forces at a time of pressing demand for increased munition production. To encourage women to join the workforce, Lloyd George, now Minister of Munitions, liaised with the WSPU. Enmities between the two were quickly overcome. Demonstrations, largely financed by Lloyd George and co-ordinated by the WSPU, were organised to publicise the need for women to join the labour force. For example, the WSPU was given £2,000 to stage a 'women's right to serve' march (known as The Great Procession of Women), on 17th July 1915. In the Midlands the WSPU organised 'At Homes' and meetings outside large factories to gain support for the war effort.

The jingoism of the leaders of the WSPU verged on the extreme. Shedding their subversive, and somewhat anarchistic, role of the pre-war years, the suffragettes became the archest of arch-patriots. In 1915 the suffragettes renamed their paper *Britannia* to express their commitment to the British Empire, and in November 1917 the name of the WSPU was changed to the Women's Party. Emmeline and

Christabel Pankhurst were great assets in promoting the war effort world-wide: they launched a campaign to urge Russian women to encourage their men to keep fighting and toured America and Canada to speak on women and war service. At home, they called for military conscription for men, industrial conscription for women and the abolition of trade unions. Any young man wearing civilian dress who was unfortunate enough to encounter Emmeline Pankhurst and her supporters was handed a white feather as a symbol of cowardice. Furthermore, the WSPU demanded that conscientious objectors, alongside those of the enemy race living in Britain, be interned.

Yet not all WSPU members agreed with the Pankhurst pronouncements and their use of WSPU funds to promote the war effort. As a consequence, two different groups split from the WSPU to form their own suffrage organisations: the Suffragettes of the Women's Social and Political Union (SWSPU) in October 1915 and the Independent Women's Social and Political Union (IWSPU) in March 1916. Unfortunately, apart from a brief mention in a few books, these groups have largely been ignored by historians. However, each group produced its own paper, the *Suffragette News Sheet* and *The Independent Suffragette*, which provide some opportunities for historical research.

b) The East London Federation of Suffragettes

In marked contrast to her flag-waving relatives, Sylvia Pankhurst condemned the war as an imperialistic venture, supported conscientious objection, adhered to her socialist principles and emerged as 'one of Britain's leading revolutionary anti-war agitators'.[3] At times the ELFS even preached sedition. 'We believe that the conscientious objector who refuses to become a soldier, the soldiers who establish a truce in the trenches, and the people which forces its Government to make peace, are all fighting the same fight'.[4] In the midst of war the ELFS published a letter from the leader of the Social Democrats in Germany, Karl Liebkneckt, urging suffragettes to fight both for the vote and for peace. Sylvia Pankhurst also participated in a Women's Peace Conference at the Hague and was elected to the Executive Committee of the Women's International League. By the end of the war she was a fully fledged revolutionary socialist who believed that only a complete change in society could herald equality between the sexes. She, and her organisation, even applauded the Bolshevik revolution in Russia because 'the capitalist system of society is irreconcilable with the freedom and the just demands of the workers'.[5] The ELFS urged the abolition of capitalism and called for the establishment of a Socialist Commonwealth in which the means of production and distribution would be employed in the interests of the people. It is therefore not surprising that in 1916 the ELFS first changed its name to the Workers' Suffrage Federation and later in 1918 to the Workers' Socialist Federation with a corresponding change in their newspaper title from *The Women's Dreadnought* to *The Workers' Dreadnought* in 1917.

Throughout the war the ELFS campaigned for civil liberties, the control of food prices and profits, for the nationalisation of the food supply and against rising prices for food. Towards the end of the war it demanded the abolition of private profit, the socialisation of food and even suggested that food be supplied free, paid for by the rates. The plight of working-class women also concerned the ELFS and much of its effort revolved around improving their lives. The ELFS campaigned for better rates of pay in charitable organisations such as Queen Mary's Workshops; sent petitions, demonstrations and deputations concerning pay and conditions in munitions factories to Lloyd George; and supported equal pay for equal work, arguing that it was 'vitally important that every woman shall refuse to do a man's work unless she gets a man's pay'.[6] When the Government introduced Regulation 40D (which made it a crime for women with venereal disease to have, or even suggest to have, sexual intercourse with anyone in the armed forces), the ELFS, along with other feminist groups, unsuccessfully, opposed it.

The war brought distress to soldiers' wives and dependants and so the ELFS campaigned widely on their behalf. In 1914 it protested against the 'Cessation of Separation Allowances and of Allotments of Pay to the Unworthy', which threatened to discontinue the allowances of women found guilty of misconduct, immorality or child neglect. In 1915, along with the local Labour MP, George Lansbury, the ELFS also formed the League of Rights for Soldiers and Sailors' Wives and Relatives to fight for an increase in the separation allowances paid to women whose husbands were away fighting.

From the evidence charted above, and the fact that it was a tiny organisation, it is difficult to believe that the government wished to reward the ELFS for their emphatically negative reaction to the war. However, in much of its practice, the ELFS mirrored the work of other suffrage organisations by focusing on relief work. For much of the time Sylvia Pankhurst acted as social worker rather than working socialist. She, and her organisation, opened an unemployment bureau and set up a toy and boot factory to help the unemployed. The ELFS set up five centres in the East End of London, which offered free milk to mothers and a nurse to advise on the health of their babies, and converted an old pub called the Gunmakers' Arms into a nursery, renaming it the Mothers' Arms. A cost price restaurant was also opened which offered dinner at 2d, well below the price charged by local restaurants. This restaurant was used regularly by East Enders but it was often criticised because the food it served - such as unpeeled potatoes and unpeeled turnips - although healthy, looked unappetising.

c) The National Union of Women's Suffrage Societies

Meanwhile the NUWSS was bitterly divided over the war. While there were some members who wholeheartedly supported the war effort, there were others who were ambivalent and still others who were unwilling to support it at all. Millicent Fawcett represented the first group believing that 'a wholesome internationalism could rest only on a wholesome nationalism'.[7] Although she had signed an appeal for peace at the beginning of August 1914 she changed her mind a few days later when war broke out and declared 'Women, your country needs you.' War, she believed, was the gravest crisis facing Britain for if Germany won it would destroy the democratic institution of Parliament. Nonetheless, Millicent Fawcett 'was no flag waving jingoist; she opposed the idea of giving white feathers ... regretted the need for conscription and repudiated vulgar anti-German feeling'.[8] Indeed, she regretted the war but felt it impolitic to implicate suffrage with the controversy over pacifism versus patriotism.

Not all members of the NUWSS agreed with Millicent Fawcett, preferring to retain their identity as suffragists rather than be swept away by a wave of chauvinism. Eventually these disagreements led to a division in the NUWSS, especially when it refused official recognition to an international Peace Conference for women held at The Hague. Millicent Fawcett, in particular, refused to associate the NUWSS with the conference because she feared that its reputation would be damaged if it was associated with pacifism. In the end all the national officers, apart from Millicant Fawcett and the Treasurer, resigned to form the Women's International League for Peace and Freedom.

Whatever their attitude towards the war almost all of the suffragists were active in wartime relief work. Indeed relief work overcame some of the divisions within the NUWSS and strengthened the bonds between the remaining membership. One of the first tasks of the NUWSS was to establish a register of voluntary workers, who would in turn find the unemployed suitable work. When war broke out there was a dramatic increase in female unemployment as many of the industries such as dressmaking, which employed large numbers of women, virtually collapsed as richer women cut back on their purchase of luxury goods. Industries such as the cotton trade, when the German market ended, and the fishery trade, when the North Sea was closed to shipping, also collapsed leaving many women out of work. By September 1914 over 44 per cent of women were unemployed.

In response to this high female unemployment, members of the NUWSS set to work organising the unemployed and soon became the major focus of relief work in many cities and towns. In Birmingham, it opened a workroom where garments were made for war relief and a dining room for pregnant and nursing mothers as well as establishing women patrols to 'protect the honour of young girls' and guard against prostitution. At the outbreak of war the Dundee branch offered to help the city council alleviate poverty and distress caused by war; similarly the Edinburgh and Glasgow branches undertook relief work. In London, it established a Women's Service Bureau which worked with Belgian refugees, War Relief Committees, Red Cross Units, Hospital Stores and Canteens.

By 1915 there was a shortage of workers, so the NUWSS set up an employment register and interviewed women to replace men sent to the front. For example, the first 80 munition workers at the Woolwich Arsenal were recruited by the London Society, as were supervisors and workers for munition factories all over Britain. Training schools, such as that for oxyacetylene welding at Notting Hill, were also opened by the London branch to supply workers for the aircraft industry.

One of the most important initiatives of the NUWSS was the setting up and financing of Scottish Women's Hospitals Units. These units employed all-female teams of doctors, nurses and ambulance drivers to work on the front lines of the war in some of the worst of the fighting zones. By 1915 there were five medical units operating in Corsica, France, Salonika and Serbia. The NUWSS also provided medical relief to the civilian populations of Europe who had been disturbed by the upheaval of war. Under a predominantly Quaker aegis, maternity and children's hospitals were set up for refugees and sanatoria for tuberculosis sufferers.

Unlike the WSPU, the NUWSS remained committed to women's suffrage and left its organisational structure intact, enabling it to recommence suffrage activities when the time was right. Indeed the NUWSS used the same staff and organising facilities for its relief work as it had for the vote. Some branches, such as Birmingham's, never lost sight of the suffrage cause and held meetings and demonstrations and drafted petitions to promote votes for women. This was significant, for whenever the franchise question was raised in the House of Commons the NUWSS were well placed to lobby trade unions, municipal authorities, the press and the Government in support of women's suffrage. More importantly, the hard work of both the suffragettes and the suffragists during the war ended the spectre of militancy and conferred respectability on the suffrage cause. It was thought that the women involved in the suffrage movement had shown themselves to be responsible and mature beings who were more than capable of taking part in the democracy which they had defended.

2 Women's War Work and the Vote

When women were enfranchised in 1918 billboards announced that 'The Nation Thanks the Women'. A grateful nation, overwhelmed by the sacrifices of munition workers in particular, granted them suffrage as recompense for their efforts. It was also supposed that women were enfranchised because the war had changed masculine perceptions about women's role in society. For the first time women were accepted into the public world of work which led, ultimately, to their acceptance in the public world of politics.

From the outset women of all social classes were absorbed into the war effort and played a crucial part on the Home Front. Many upper-class and middle-class women experienced their first taste of paid work during the war, entering occupations that would have been deemed unsuitable in peacetime. Aristocratic women were found in the higher echelons, advising government departments on health and employment, heading Food Economy Campaigns, and presiding over the newly formed women's armed services. Lady Londonderry, for example, became the first Colonel in Chief of the Women's Volunteer Reserve in February 1915. Two years later, when the Land Army was formed, women from upper- and middle-class backgrounds joined as agricultural workers. (Selection boards usually turned down working-class women who volunteered for the Land Army because they were believed to lack the high moral fibre needed for farm life.) On the farm, women were expected to do a wide variety of jobs such as ploughing, planting and harvesting as well as look after the sheep and other animals.

Other women joined the Women's Auxiliary Army Corps (WAACS) which had been formed in 1916, the Women's Royal Naval Service (WRENS), or the Women's Royal Air Force (WRAFS), set up in 1918. Most women who joined the auxiliary armed forces worked in a supportive capacity, as drivers, messengers, typists, telephonists and storekeepers but some did receive technical training. A few WRAFS were employed as welders and carpenters to work on aeroplanes but none actually flew so they were called penguins: birds who cannot fly. The *Daily Express* once suggested that flying should not be a woman's job because they would lose their heads in an emergency! Although not officially enlisted, these women were considered part of the regular British Army. And at the very least, as Martin Pugh notes, the war disposed of one old argument against votes for women - the one that women were incapable of taking part in the defence of the country. In this respect women played a large part in the national defence - at least on the home front - and were thus entitled to the political rewards that followed from it.

Upper-class women also joined the Voluntary Aid Attachments (VAD), formed in 1909 but greatly expanded during the war, to nurse injured soldiers both at home and at the front. These women have often been portrayed romantically as heroines who sacrificed their privileged upbringing to nurse the sick and wounded. Vera Brittain (a famous writer and mother of former MP Shirley Williams), who was about to go to Oxford when war was declared, wrote about her experiences as a young VAD gazing 'half-hypnotized, at the dishevelled beds, the stretchers on the floor, the scattered boots and piles of muddy khaki, the brown blankets turned back from smashed limbs bound to splints by filthy blood-stained bandages. Beneath each stinking wad of sodden wool and gauze an obscene horror waited for me.'[9] Criticism was sometimes made of these middle-class girls who spent a morning at the hospital whilst domestic servants cleaned their homes. For instance, when Vera Brittain was at the front nursing soldiers, her mother employed domestic servants to look after their home. Nevertheless, these nurses generally received a sympathetic press and were seen to deserve the vote.

Unlike most of their upper- and middle-class colleagues, working-class women did not go out to work because of the war. They had to work anyway. However, war did change the nature of their occupation. War offered an alternative to the grossly exploitative job of domestic service or sweated labour. In fact domestic service diminished by 400,000 during the war, reducing from 1,658,000 to 1,258,000. At railway stations there were women porters, ticket collectors and guards. Women replaced men as bus drivers, window cleaners, chimney sweeps, coal deliverers, street sweepers, electricians and fire-fighters as the rather posed photograph on page 96 shows. By 1917 bus conductresses had gone up from a half a dozen to about 2,500 and transport workers increased from 18,000 in 1914 to 117,000 in 1918. Munitions obviously showed the biggest increase in female labour. In 1914, Woolwich Arsenal employed 125 women in 1914 whereas by 1917 over 25,000 women worked there.

It was the munition worker who captured the imagination of the press and the general public. Munition workers performed a variety of jobs, ranging from filling shells and making bullets to assembling detonators. Their hours were long - sometimes 14 hours a day for weeks on end - and their conditions of work known to be dangerous. TNT poisoning, which turned the skin yellow, thus earning the women the nickname of 'Canary Girls', was an occupational hazard. In Woolwich Arsenal about 37 per cent of the women suffered from stomach pain, nausea and constipation as a result of TNT poisoning. Other symptoms included skin rashes, giddiness, drowsiness, swelling of hands and feet. In 1916 the first deaths from toxic jaundice were reported but little was done. Working in a munition factory was also highly dangerous because of the risk of explosion. Safety measures were taken to avoid accidents: each woman had to hand over all personal belongings such as matches, cigarettes, wedding rings and other jewellery before they entered the shell filling section. Women wore protective clothes without any metal zips in them, garters rather than suspender belts and caps to tie up long hair as metal hair grips were banned. In spite of these precautions accidents were common. The most notorious was that of Silvertown in the East End of London in 1917 where a number of women were killed in an horrific explosion.

Women firefighters in the First World War

3 War, Suffrage and the Government

It is important, of course, to examine women's suffrage and war from the perspective of parliamentary politics. For over 50 years before the war an all-male Parliament was reluctant to enfranchise women and yet by the close of war in 1918 politicians had changed their minds. The reasons for the shifts which took place in Government thinking between 1914 and 1918 therefore need consideration.

Firstly, and perhaps most importantly, there was a need for franchise reform in general. The existing franchise law required men who qualified as householders to have occupied a dwelling for at least a year prior to an election. Large numbers of the armed forces were thus ineligible to vote because they no longer held or had never held a 12 month residency. And a significant minority of men, who had risked their lives fighting in the front lines, had never ever been enfranchised. This, of course, would not do. In 1916, an all party conference, composed of MPs from both the House of Commons and the House of Lords presided over by the Speaker of the House of

Commons, was appointed to draft a proposal on the franchise and registration. The Speaker's Conference, as it was known, took place behind closed doors, no evidence was gathered and no lobbying accepted. The debate was conducted without any contribution from women - at least officially. Fortunately for women, there were many supporters of women's suffrage within the Speaker's Conference, so votes for women was assured of a sympathetic hearing. Nevertheless, although only a limited number of women were granted the vote (see page 1) because it was feared that they might swamp the male elec-torate, over eight million women were enfranchised.

Secondly, there were a number of key changes in Parliament which altered the balance between those who opposed and those who were in favour of votes for women. The entry into Government of several suffragist MPs augured well for the success of any women's suffrage amendment. Balfour, Bonar Law and Arthur Henderson, all of whom supported suffrage, were also promoted to the Cabinet replacing men who were antagonistic. More importantly Lloyd George, who was (more or less) sympathetic to women's suffrage, replaced Asquith as Prime Minister in December 1916.

Thirdly, the war allowed a number of hostile MPs - Asquith in particular - the excuse to climb down from their, now untenable, position of opposing votes for women. These MPs, although not fully converted to women's suffrage, realised that reform was inevitable so used women's war work as a pretext to recant and save face. Women, it was argued, had demonstrated that they were mature and sensible enough by their significant contribution towards the war effort to be rewarded with the vote. As Asquith stated, somewhat disengenuously given his previous comments about women's suffrage, in 1917:

1 Why, and in what sense, the House may ask, have I changed my views?
   … My opposition to woman suffrage has always been based, and
   based solely, on considerations of public expediency. I think that
   some years ago I ventured to use the expression 'Let the women
5 work out their own salvation'. Well, Sir, they have … How could we
   have carried on the War without them? There is hardly a service in
   which women have not been at least as active as men … But what
   moves me more in this matter is the problem of reconstruction
   when the war is over. The questions which will arise with regard to
10 women's labour and women's functions are questions in which I find
   it impossible to withhold from women, the power and the right of
   making their voices heard. And let me add that, since the War began,
   now nearly three years ago, we have had no recurrence of that
   detestable campaign which disfigured the annals of political agitation
15 in this country, and no one can now contend that we are yielding to
   violence what we refused to concede to argument.

But his remarks concerning the female electorate of Paisley in 1920 suggest that he still resented women's involvement in parliamentary politics:

> There are about fifteen thousand women on the Register - a dim, impenetrable lot, for the most part hopelessly ignorant of politics, credulous to the last degree, and flickering with gusts of sentiment like a candle in the wind.

Fourthly, in May 1915 the Liberal Government evolved into a Coalition government. The resulting decline in the importance of party divisions offered the prospect of all party agreement on women's suffrage. As Brian Harrison points out, women's suffrage supporters were no longer fragmented between two, and sometimes three, political parties.

Furthermore, the old fears that one party might benefit from women's suffrage were laid to rest. The enfranchisement of some eight million women did not present an advantage to any one political party. On the one hand, both the Liberals and the Labour Party thought that the new proposed female electorate was much too large and socially mixed to give any advantage to the Conservatives. On the other hand, the Conservatives recognised that by this time adult male suffrage was unavoidable and so had little to lose - and perhaps something to gain - by women over 30, who were thought to be politically moderate, being included. The fact that munition workers in the main were excluded from the vote was also significant in gaining Conservative support. Munition workers were of course predominantly working-class and might have voted Labour. Women's suffrage was therefore a compromise: no party got what it wanted. Like other reform Acts it was illogical - there was no rational justification for excluding younger women, especially when male conscripts of 19 received the vote. Nonetheless, the compromise worked because it maximised support which a more radical proposal of universal suffrage might not.

Finally, Britain was merely reflecting an international trend towards full democracy. Women in New Zealand, Australia, Finland, Denmark and Norway had already been enfranchised women. Canada (except Quebec) had granted votes for women in 1917 as had four American states. And just as the debate was taking place on women's suffrage in Britain the American House of Representatives carried votes for women by a two-thirds majority (even though it was not ratified until August 1920). It would have been a peculiar political embarrassment if the mother of democracy, Britain, lagged behind those of other countries.

As a consequence, when the division bell sounded in the House of Commons, 385 MPs voted in favour and 55 against the clause in the Representation of the People Bill supporting votes for women. The Bill then passed smoothly through the Lords largely because Lord Curzon, member of the Coalition Government and President of the

League for Opposing Woman Suffrage, encouraged pe
from voting if they could not support it. And so on Febr
votes for women - after more than 60 years of campaigr
to end all wars - was at last achieved.

4 Conclusion

It would be naive to believe that women received the vote solely for
services rendered in the First World War. It must be remembered that
only women over 30 were given the vote (see page 1) and they were
not the ones who had made the most substantial contribution towards
the war. Indeed the very women who had helped in the war effort - the
young women of the munitions factories in particular - were actually
denied the vote. As Martin Pugh has noted, the vote - just like the
Second Reform Act - was conferred on the respectable and the
responsible. It was felt unlikely that the mature and married female
would commit themselves to radical demands or revolutionary
change but instead would help promote social stability amongst
younger women.

The significance of women's war work in the achievement of the
vote is therefore perhaps not as great as first assumed. In reality,
women were greatly resented in both agriculture and industry
because, even though they received more money than perhaps they
had ever earned before, they still undercut male wages. There was a
great fear that the concept of the family wage (where a man was paid
sufficient to keep a wife and children) was being eroded and that low
paid and unskilled women workers would peg wages below acceptable
levels. Male trade unionists were far from enthusiastic about women
joining a union to increase their rates of pay. It is true that a few
unions encouraged women to join but many, like the Amalgamated
Society of Engineers, excluded or ignored them. Thus five-sixths of
women workers remained outside the unions during war time. Even
on an individual level there was hostility from male workers.
Engineering workers, such as those at Vickers, objected to setting up
machines for women working in the factory. Men 'froze out' women
workers, gave them no assistance, incorrect instructions and even
sabotaged their work. In one incident a women had her desk drawer
nailed up while, another time, oil was poured over the contents.
Farmers too disliked women workers and preferred to employ young
boys or old age pensioners, arguing that women lacked the strength
for the more strenuous farm jobs such as ploughing.

Women's jobs in these new found industries were not, and were
never meant to be, permanent. As men returned from fighting in the
trenches they wanted their jobs back in the factories, in transport and
in offices. In 1918 a trade union conference called for women to be
banned from 'unsuitable' trades, for their hours to be regulated and
for the exclusion of married women from work. In 1920 unemployed

ex-servicemen in Bristol smashed the windows of tram cars and attacked female conductresses in protest at women working. And when women resisted returning to domestic service they found their unemployment benefit withdrawn and were criticised in the press as 'slackers with state pay'. Not surprisingly, by 1921 most women had left their wartime jobs.

Moreover, women may well not have been granted the vote if the suffragists and suffragettes had not campaigned so effectively before the war. Undoubtedly, the pre-war suffrage movement prepared the ground for votes for women. French women, for example, were not enfranchised despite their participation in the war effort, largely because there had been no women's suffrage movement pre-war. Furthermore, it seemed likely that the women's suffrage movement would recommence once the war had ended with perhaps a renewal of the militancy which had plagued previous governments. One can only assume that, because the political climate was very different in 1918 than it had been in 1914, it would be inconceivable for the Government to imprison those self-same women who had so publicly participated in the war effort. As Morgan suggests 'it was clear that the killing of Suffrage by any method would lead to a dangerous reversion to massive dissatisfaction among thousands of women whom publicly politicians were praising for their war efforts'[10], especially at a time of widespread strikes and of fear of Bolshevism.

In many ways, the war may have delayed the franchise rather than expedited it. Just before the outbreak of war there were conciliatory gestures by key MPs: Asquith received deputations from the NUWSS and the ELFS; Sir John Simon emerged as a cabinet supporter; and Lloyd George offered a place on his platform to suffrage speakers. There was also evidence to suggest that the Liberal Party was pressurising prospective MPs to support women's suffrage and replacing those unsympathetic to the suffrage cause with those who agreed with it. Holton argues that 'only two weeks before the outbreak of war, negotiations between suffragists and government were taking place'.[11] In addition, the Liberal leadership seemed ready to make women's suffrage part of its party programme. This of course is mere speculation. Negotiations between the government and women's suffragists had taken place many times before but had never provided votes for women. There was no guarantee that it would have been the case this time.

Of course, neither the view that women achieved the vote because of their pre-war campaigns nor the view that women achieved the vote because of the war is ultimately sustainable. As with most historical judgements, there are a number of reasons for such a significant event and historians much prefer a synthesis of causes to crude over-simplification. It must also be remembered that the vote was still not entirely won as full adult universal suffrage was not achieved until 1928.

References
1   Gifford Lewis, *Eva Gore Booth and Esther Roper* (Pandora, 1988), pp. 165-6.
2   Brian Harrison, *Prudent Revolutionaries* (Clarendon Press, 1987), p. 35.
3   Barbara Winslow, *Sylvia Pankhurst* (UCL, 1996), p. 76.
4   *Workers Dreadnought,* August 17th, 1917.
5   Ibid, June 2nd, 1917.
6   *Woman's Dreadnought,* February 13th, 1915.
7   Brian Harrison, *Prudent Revolutionaries,* p. 18.
8   Ibid.
9   Vera Brittain, *Testament of Youth* (Virago, 1992), p. 410.
10 D. Morgan, *Suffragists and Liberals* (Blackwell, 1975), p. 143.
11 Sandra Stanley Holton, *Suffrage and Democracy* (Cambridge University Press, 1986), p. 125.

Source-based questions on 'Women, Suffrage and the First World War'

1. Asquith's comments on women's suffrage
Read the comments made by Asquith about women's suffrage on pages 97 and 98.
a)   What does Asquith mean by 'no one can now contend that we are yielding to violence what we refused to concede to argument' (line 15-16)? (4 marks)
b)   Does the second source reveal anything about Asquith's attitude towards women's suffrage? Give reasons for your answer. (4 marks)
c)   How does Asquith's thinking, as reflected in the two sources, accord with his and his party's actions? (7 marks)

Answering essay questions on 'Women, Suffrage and the First World War'

Examiners, like most historians, are concerned above all with the issue of causation, or in other words, why something happened. It is therefore possible to group the majority of questions about women's suffrage under the heading: why did women obtain the vote? Examiners may ask this in a variety of ways but essentially it is the same question and requires the use of similar content. For example:
1.   Why was women's suffrage so long delayed?
2.   Did the militant campaigns of the suffragettes obstruct the cause they sought to promote?
3.   Discuss the various interpretations put forward by historians as to why women gained the vote in 1918.
4.   'If anyone is asked who won the vote for British women, the name of Pankhurst is more likely to be voiced than any other' (Brian Harrison). Discuss.

5. How important were the suffragists in gaining the vote for women?
6. To what extent was the enactment of women's suffrage one of the surprises of the 1914-18 War?
7. 'Nothing seems more natural and inevitable at first glance than that women should have won the vote in the First World War' (Martin Pugh). Discuss.
8. Was the highly skilled and dangerous work done by women during the war the greatest factor in the granting of the vote to women?

All of these questions require you to be aware of the main reasons why women were enfranchised, that is, the significance of both the suffragist and the suffragette campaigns before the war and the impact of war on the suffrage movement. You will find all of the chapters in this book (and others!) relevant in answering questions and constructing arguments around these particular issues.

For example question (8) is really a 'on the one hand, on the other hand' question in which you should attempt some balanced judgement. Examiners are looking for your understanding of the arguments either for or against. 'On the one hand' you will need to be aware of the important role that munition workers played in the First World War, working in dangerous conditions for long hours. This, along with other women's contribution to the war effort, was highly praised and women workers overall received favourable press coverage which in turn convinced people that they were capable of voting responsibly. 'On the other hand' it is important to remember that large numbers of munition workers were not given the vote as they were under the age of 30. Moreover, the war itself transformed not only the lives of women but the political situation. The hostile Government of Asquith was not only replaced by leaders more sympathetic towards female suffrage but the war had highlighted the need to transform the electoral register. Furthermore, most of the women's suffrage movement worked with the Government to ensure victory in war rather than continue campaigning for their own needs. In these circumstances, women's suffrage was likely to succeed. Usually highest marks are given for balanced answers but there are questions which require students to reach a conclusion. There is therefore no need to 'sit on the fence' as you could gain a good grade by arguing a one-sided case. However, in most of these essays you should demonstrate a good understanding of both sides of the argument and show why you find one argument more persuasive than the other. Here it is essential that you understand the status of the judgements you make.

On the whole, however, women's suffrage would not have succeeded without the consistent campaigning of the pre-war years. From the mid-1860s, suffragists had chosen a variety of methods with which to persuade the government and the rest of the country of the justice of their cause. Fearful perhaps of a return to the militancy of the Edwardian period, the Government included women in a franchise reform bill. Even so, women did not receive the vote on the same terms as men until 1928.

Summary Diagram
Women, Suffrage and the First World War

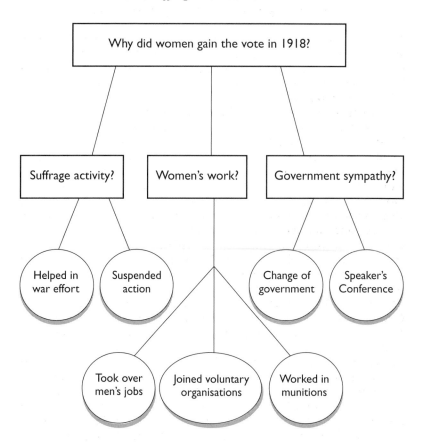

7 Conclusion: Life after Suffrage

So was it all worth it? Did the vote bring about the changes that the suffragists and suffragettes yearned for? Many certainly thought so. Historians, of course, are more circumspect than suffrage activists because with hindsight they are able to evaluate the causes and consequences of significant historical events more clearly. From this vantage point, historians of the suffrage movement can assess whether the franchise accomplished what those who energetically campaigned for it desired, or whether the vote marked the end of women's achievements. However, controversy is also at the heart of history and so, not surprisingly, historians differ on the effect that the vote had on women's lives, especially since the consequences of votes for women, are in many ways, still working themselves out.

1 The Effect of the Vote

At first suffragists, elated at the prospect of voting, insisted that the vote had a tremendous significance for women's rights. To their minds, the enfranchisement of women would revolutionise government thinking as the voting power of the new electorate could not be ignored:

> The Representation of the People Act had not been on the Statute Book a fortnight before the House of Commons discovered that every Bill which came before it had a 'woman's side', and the Party Whips began eagerly to ask 'what the women thought'. The precincts
> 5 of the House of Commons, which had been firmly closed to all women since the early days of the militant agitation, were now opened, and access to Members became wonderfully easy. Letters from women constituents no longer went straight into waste-paparbaskets but received elaborate answers, and the agents of the
> 10 women's societies were positively welcomed at Westminster.[1]

Historians Martin Pugh and Olive Banks share this optimism and claim that, because of their newly acquired voting power, women achieved considerable gains. According to Pugh, there were 21 pieces of legislation between 1918 and 1929 which concerned women and 'it would be hard to find any comparable concentration before or since'.[2] Given these achievements, it is tempting to adopt a Whiggish approach to votes for women and represent women's advancements as an inevitable evolutionary process. History, however, is a little untidier and more of a roller coaster - with its ups and downs - than a straight railway track which runs relentlessly onwards to its destination. Women held extravagant hopes for what the vote could achieve as there were numerous setbacks as well as successes. In fact, another group of historians believe that women did not benefit from the vote politically, economically or socially. They hold that any advances made by women in this period were due to post-war feminist campaigning and to the continuation of Edwardian Liberalism, which was sympathetic to social reform, rather than the consequences of women's franchise.

a) Effects on Parliament

In 1918, for the first time in legal and political history, women had the opportunity to participate equally in the democratic process. Britain could now claim that she had a representative government as electoral democracy was no longer the preserve of men. After many years of struggle, Britain allegedly had a just and balanced government as the majority of the population was now enfranchised. The 1918 Representation Act may well have been the last great reform act, but these views must be approached with some caution as women aged between 21 and 30 were still denied the vote. Not until 1928 did women receive the vote on the same terms as men, thus properly marking the beginning of modern democracy in Britain (see page 1).

Women may well have voted but they were slow in taking their places in the House of Commons. In the first election, in December 1918, 17 women, including a number of suffragists and suffragettes, stood for Parliament. All but one of the female candidates were defeated at the polls, including Christabel Pankhurst who stood as Conservative candidate for Smethwick and Emmeline Pethick Lawrence who stood as a Labour candidate in Manchester. The only woman to be elected was Constance Markievicz who, because she stood as a Sinn Fein member, (whose policy at the time was not to recognise the British Government or its mechanisms), refused to take her seat. Ironically, the first woman MP to take her seat in the House of Commons (Nancy Astor) got there when her husband, who had been Conservative MP for Plymouth, was elevated to the peerage. Until then Nancy Astor had not been interested in running for office but because Plymouth was regarded as the family seat of the Astors she was willing to take over from her husband.

Nancy Astor was the exception rather than the rule. In 1922 only 33 women were nominated as Parliamentary candidates out of a possible 615. By 1929 this had risen to 69, but it was hardly a significant figure especially when four out of five women stood in constituencies known to be hopeless for their particular parties and therefore had little chance of winning. Moreover, ten out of the 36 women who actually became MPs in this period gained their seats at by-elections rather than general elections, which suggests that their success may have as much to do with arbitrary factors such as voter dissatisfaction as with support for specifically female candidates. Furthermore, several Conservative women MPs owed their success, like Nancy Astor, to family connections rather than to feminist pressure.

Most women had the legal right to become MPs but social convention generally denied them the opportunity. Women's role in 1920, as in 1860, was still perceived to be in their own house looking after their family not in the House of Commons looking after the country. As a consequence, local constituencies, fearing that women might alienate the electorate, were unwilling to accept them as prospective MPs. Indeed, Conservative selection Committees looked for husband and wife teams with men - of course - as MPs and women acting in a supportive capacity, organising fêtes and bazaars to raise money and entertaining the party faithful.

Furthermore, the enfranchisement of women did not change the nature of Parliamentary politics. Suffragists and suffragettes had hoped that once women achieved the vote they would make a distinctive contribution to the political arena by 'feminising' politics. It was believed that women would bring special skills to Parliament which would make the confrontational style of party politics disappear in favour of politics based on principles. This wish was not fulfilled. The House of Commons remained 'essentially a man's institution evolved through centuries by men to deal with men's affairs in a man's way'.[3] Men not only dominated numerically in the House of Commons but so too did their style of politics. The election of women MPs neither brought about a new age nor 'feminised' the political process, as women merely adapted to the masculine style of the House of Commons, learning debating skills and an adversarial approach. Overall, women MPs failed to make a distinctive stand over women's issues but took party political sides just like the men. Even women MPs with feminist sympathies were forced to compromise their feminism or else become marginalised within party politics. As Pugh has pointed out, 'few of the female party politicians were willing or able to use their influence within their party' to promote women's concerns. However, the reluctance of women MPs to promote women's issues may have been because they remained a small minority: who knows what significant numbers of women MPs may now do?

b) Effects on Women's Work

Suffragists and suffragettes had wanted the vote partly to widen women's employment opportunities, increase their pay and improve their working conditions. To some extent they had their wishes fulfilled, at least in the legal sense. In 1919, as a direct result of women's franchise, the Sex Disqualification Removal Act stated that 'a person should not be disqualified by sex or marriage from the exercise of any public function or from being appointed or holding any civil or judicial office or post or from entering or assuming or carrying on any civil profession or vocation'. This allowed women to take up civil service and judicial posts, become barristers or magistrates and serve on juries. This Act opened the legal profession to women like Christabel Pankhurst who had studied law but had not been allowed to practise it except in her own defence. It also allowed women to become chartered accountants and bankers. Certainly in the 1920s there were a number of significant firsts: the first woman to qualify as a veterinary surgeon; the first woman pilot to enter an air race; the first female British delegate to the League of Nations; the first woman solicitor; the first woman barrister; the first jurywomen; the first female JP; and the first woman deacon in the Church of England.

Women may have been granted the legal right to enter previously male professions but they made insignificant inroads. Despite the vote, most work was as much characterised by a sexual division of labour in 1928 as it had been over 60 years before. Many professions continued to be male-dominated. In 1919 many of the London teaching hospitals still refused to train women doctors; in 1920 when the Civil Service was re-organised women remained excluded from high office; and by 1927 only a small number of women had been appointed as JPs. Greater opportunities emerged for middle-class women in the teaching and clerical professions but women were rarely given the top jobs. As one President of the National Association of Schoolmasters declared in 1934, 'Only a nation heading for a madhouse would force upon men ... such a position as service under a spinster headmistress.'[4] And when the expansion of the white-blouse worker - the department store shop assistant, the nurse and the clerk - offered women employment opportunities this owed more to technological and educational advances than to the vote.

Moreover, employers often ignored the 1919 Sexual Disqualif-ication Removal Act and obliged women to resign when they married. In the 1920s about three-quarters of all local authorities operated a marriage bar for women teachers and many public health authorities dismissed married female doctors and nurses; similarly women civil servants were given a dowry and forced to leave once they married. The decision not to employ married women was justified because 'women could not service two masters'[5], that is their husbands and their bosses, at the same time. In the eyes of many men, women's only legitimate reason for existence was to serve them, so little had changed in this respect.

Votes for women also did little for working-class women as there continued to be a high degree of sexual segregation in working-class occupations. Domestic service and agricultural labour remained the only two options available to working-class rural women until well after the Second World War. Once again, even when women worked in the same areas as men, they were found in the lower grades of these occupations, being over-represented in unskilled rather than skilled jobs. New opportunities did occur for women in the new light indus-tries but these, like those of the white blouse workers, were the effect of technological change rather than the effect of the vote.

More importantly, women remained a cheap and easily exploitable workforce as their work commanded lower rates of pay than men, whether they were middle-class or working-class. Despite a campaign to obtain equal pay, female teachers' salaries were set one fifth lower than men's by the Standing Joint Committee on Teachers' Salaries. Similarly women civil servants were paid 75 per cent of male salaries as a rule. In all-female middle-class occupations women were worse off. Nursing, for example, was seen as a vocation rather than a career, so women were paid low salaries in order to attract middle-class women who did not need to work for a living. Working-class women fared little better, for they continued to receive wages roughly half of that of men.

One is therefore led to believe that although women had gained political power through the ballot box, economic power was still held by men. The justification for this inequality can be traced to the ideology of domesticity whereby women were perceived as wives and mothers rather than workers. Indeed, Martin Pugh claims that it was commonly held that working women deprived men of jobs - one manufacturer even advocated the dismissal of women workers in order to solve the unemployment problem. Women's pay was not surprisingly viewed as 'pin-money', and a supplement to the wages of husbands, rather than a living wage. As a consequence, women were denied the economic equality that feminists continued to demand. However, in fairness, it should be recognised that there was a consistently high level of overall unemployment in the inter-war period: unemployment never fell below one million and reached three million at its height.

c) Effects on Marriage and the Family

Post-war politicians may have promised to create homes fit for heroes but feminists wanted the same for their alleged heroines. High hopes were held that women's suffrage might not only act as a legal protection against husbands but might help promote equality in marriage. There were some notable successes in this area. Largely as a result of feminist pressure, the Matrimonial Causes Act of 1923 allowed a wife to divorce her husband on grounds of adultery, thus ending a long history of double standards for men and women. However, wives did not benefit entirely from this new legislation, as one historian suggests that it made sex more of a duty for wives than it had before. Two years later, in 1925, the Guardianship of Infants Act completed the work of nineteenth-century feminists by placing mothers and fathers in an equal position with regard to custody of their children. In the same year, husbands were no longer held responsible for any criminal act committed by their wives in their presence. In effect, this act consolidated women's position as independent beings who were outside the control and jurisdiction of their husbands.

However, the equality envisaged by the suffragists and suffragettes was still not achieved, as the removal of legal disabilities was insufficient to put women on the same footing with men. Once divorced, women who wished to stay in the marital home found they had no claim to it even though they were not the 'guilty' party. Furthermore, courts (with male judges) generally examined the conduct of women, just as much as their financial needs, before assessing their claim to maintenance.

In order to redress these economic and domestic inequalities, many feminists became concerned with 'welfare feminism' in the 1920s.[6] In 1919 the NUWSS changed its name to the National Union of Societies for Equal Citizenship (NUSEC) and, under the leadership of Eleanor Rathbone, campaigned for social reforms. Rather than struggle for equal pay with men, it was suggested that married women be given a family allowance if they cared for their children at home. In this way, women's unpaid work in the home would at last be financially recognised and rewarded. The leadership of NUSEC believed that family allowances would not only give married women some measure of financial independence but would strengthen the position of single women. With money paid directly to women with children, there would be little justification for men being paid a 'family wage' and thus more than women. Equal pay for equal work would therefore be brought about.

Not surprisingly, many feminists disagreed with this approach to women's rights. This 'new' feminism, with its emphasis on welfare at the expense of equality, was seen, for a number of reasons, as a betrayal rather than a continuation of feminism. Firstly, feminists such as Millicent Fawcett disagreed with family allowances because they consolidated, rather than challenged, women's home-making and child-rearing roles. Certainly, it broke away from the traditional feminist claim for the right of women to work outside the home for a decent wage in favour of reinforcing women's position within the family. Secondly, family allowances diverted women from the struggle for equal pay in the public world by offering them a bribe to stay at home. Thirdly, family allowances might depress working-class wages in general because the state subsidised families with children. There was therefore little incentive for employers to raise salaries in line with the cost of living. Finally, feminists dismissed family allowances as nonsense because they advocated an ideal family of three children, whereas few families were like this.

d) Effects on Sexual Morality

Suffragists and suffragettes also wanted the vote to protect young girls from sexual assault, to eliminate venereal disease, to curb unfair legislation against prostitutes, and to ensure a single moral standard for both sexes. Once again, they enjoyed only a limited success as the following evidence will show.

Feminists achieved a small victory when the 1922 Criminal Law Amendment Act abolished the 'reasonable cause to believe' clause. Under the old Act, men who had seduced a girl under sixteen were able to claim that they had not realised that she was under age and thus avoided conviction. However, the new Act was limited in scope as it only applied to full sexual intercourse and not to indecent assault.

The extent of venereal disease continued to cause alarm. Emmeline Pankhurst spent a lot of time in North America lecturing on the dangers of venereal disease, but the women's movement in Britain seemed to reserve judgement on the subject. However, the British Social Hygiene Council made strenuous efforts to curb its spread and several films were produced - 'The Girl Who Doesn't Know', 'Damaged Goods', 'The Flaw' - to educate people on the disease itself. In the 1920s Manchester City Council opened venereal clinics in public lavatories but these were quickly closed as a result of feminist and other public disapproval. And of course it was the discovery of penicillin, rather than women's moral crusading, which diminished the rate of venereal infection.

Feminist social purists certainly had friends in high places to help them establish sexual moral standards: one film censor later became President of the National Vigilance Association (a group of men and women committed to social purity) and one Home Secretary in the 1920s undertook to improve public sexual morality. As a consequence, there was rigid sexual censorship: books such as Radclyffe Hall's *Well of Loneliness* about lesbianism either faced prosecution or were not distributed and thus quietly disappeared. A woman's police force was also established to advise young girls on moral matters and investigate sex offences.

However, it could be argued that the double sexual standard, so criticised by both suffragists and suffragettes, was replaced by an even lower single standard in that there was a decline in female sexual morality rather than an improvement in male morality. Indeed, some feminists criticised the moral puritanism of the pre-war suffragettes and instead advocated women's right to sexual pleasure. As a consequence, the campaigns they led were different ones. It was believed that women could not enjoy sex because of a fear of pregnancy, so the birth control movement won favour amongst many new wave feminists. Birth control, promoted by Marie Stopes who set up the first birth control clinic in 1921 in Holloway, London, enabled women to take control of their own sexuality, or - as some feared - be as irresponsible as men.

e) Effects on the Women's Movement

Some historians claim that the women's movement declined after 1918 as few campaigners remained fully committed to extending votes for women on the same terms as men. However, this is not the case. Although the suffrage movement was not as strong as it had been pre-war, women remained active in it. Certainly, the suffragists kept up a quiet pressure on the Government throughout this time, continuously pointing out the illogicality of the 1918 decision. Yet their story still needs to be written: most historians end their work in 1918 and ignore the ten years after women gained a limited franchise. However, it is safe to say that further franchise reform was not a priority of either the feminists or the government. In many ways it was a 'tidying up' process which happened almost accidentally when a Conservative Minister gave a commitment to equal franchise during a rather lively public meeting. The Prime Minister, Baldwin, felt he should honour this promise, and fearful that if the Conservatives didn't reform the vote, Labour would, another five million young women or so were added to the voting register.

It is often argued that once women had achieved even a limited franchise in 1918, feminism lost its vital spark, its political direction and degenerated into fragmented organisations. But, as Shiela Jeffreys points out, this fails to give weight to the other concerns of feminists. Once the vote had been achieved, certain women turned their attention to other reforms. Indeed there were a myriad of organisations which either lobbied for single issue campaigns - such as the Equal Pay Campaign Committee, the Association for Moral and Social Hygiene, and the Housewives League - or which acted as an umbrella organisation, such as the National Council for Women, the National Union of Societies for Equal Citizenship and the Six Point Group. In many ways, post-war feminism, with its diverse campaigning, was the true heir of Victorian feminism.

Certainly, many leaders of the WSPU sank into political oblivion once the vote had been achieved. Christabel Pankhurst made a concerted effort to remain in the political fray by standing for the first Parliament; she then enjoyed a brief spell as a journalist before turning to Second Adventism and Christian religious revivalism. Emmeline Pankhurst led a campaign against venereal disease in Canada, set up a tea shop in the Côte d'Azur, France, before returning to stand as Conservative Parliamentary candidate for Whitechapel. But she never really became involved in the British women's movement again. Annie Kenney married in 1921 and retired from public life. 'Slasher Mary' (see page 59) joined the British Union of Fascists. Meanwhile, the leadership of the other organisations not only continued to press for universal suffrage but remained politically active in left-wing causes. Sylvia Pankhurst helped to found the British Communist Party, championed an anti-Fascist crusade and emigrated to Ethiopia. Charlotte Despard stood as Parliamentary Candidate for Battersea in the first election but her major energy was directed to working for Irish independence. She remained committed to radical socialist policies throughout the rest of her life and at the age of 91 addressed an anti-Nazi rally in Hyde Park. The Pethick Lawrences both became Labour party activists, with Fred even defeating Winston Churchill in the 1923 election. Millicent Fawcett, though no longer leader of the NUWSS, campaigned for greater work opportunities and legal justice for women. Subsequent decades, Martin Pugh argues, actually saw the waning of the impact of women's enfranchisement as the leading figures of the suffrage movement grew old and faded from the political scene. Indeed, when women finally achieved equal suffrage with men this was not followed by any further advances in women's position but this of course could have been due to the fact that Britain was about to enter a depression

It is all too easy to be cynical about the enfranchisement of women especially in view of the continuing male dominance within parliamentary politics, the continuing economic inequalities of women and the continuing conventional social expectation that women's place is in the home. Power, it is argued, no longer rests in Parliament anyway but in commerce and finance. The failure of the franchise to realise the hopes of the suffragists and the suffragettes, it is said, illustrates the limitations of the vote to effect change. Nevertheless, the franchise should not be dismissed as 'marking a cross on a piece of paper' for it not only acts as a check on government and makes those in government answerable to the electorate, but has the authority to change the economic framework of society. Governments may have failed to satisfy the demands of British feminists between the wars but the position of women in Italy and Germany, where democracy collapsed, was calamitous. Furthermore, one only has to think of the nationalisation of the 1940s, the subsequent denationalisation of the 1980s and 1990s and the Labour landslide victory of 1997 to appreciate the immense power that Parliament still enjoys. And women, who represent over 50 per cent of the electorate, certainly have the capability to change the composition of Parliament and with it the political direction of Britain. Indeed, if the 116 women MPs who were elected in 1997 have any beneficial effect, then the achievement of the vote in 1918 and 1928 will be given a new significance.

References

1 Ray Strachey, *The Cause*, p. 367.
2 M. Pugh, *The Impact of Women's Enfranchisement in Britain*, p. 321.
3 B. Harrison, *Separate Spheres*, p. 234.
4 Jane Lewis, *Women in England, 1870-1950* (Wheatsheaf, 1984), p. 190.
5 Carol Dyhouse, *Feminism and the Family in England, 1880-1929* (Basil Blackwell, 1989), p. 79.
6 Olive Banks, *Faces of Feminism* (Blackwell, 1986).

Answering essay questions on the 'Conclusion: Life after Suffrage'

Essays which examine the effects of an event reflect another major concern of historians: consequence. What was the result or the effect of any particular course of action? Of course, it is extremely difficult to calculate the effects of any legislative change, especially since there are so many other factors which may play a part, but this should not stop us from trying to assess the impact of the vote on women's lives. Questions may be phrased in a number of ways but the key issues are whether or not women actually benefitted from the franchise or whether their lives remained the same.

1. To what extent did women benefit as a result of the franchise between 1918 and 1928?
2. 'Today our assessment of the impact of women's enfranchisement in Britain must still be provisional'. Discuss.
3. Did votes for women promise more than it achieved?
4. Compare and contrast women's lives before and after the vote was won.

Answers to question (1) could draw directly upon the notes in the diagram and a plan could be as follows:

Introduction: Present the argument that women only partially benefited from the vote

Paragraph one: examine the effect of politics

Paragraph two: examine the nature of women's work

Paragraph three: examine women's role in the family

Paragraph four: examine the effect of social purity on women's lives

Conclusion: sum up the main points and perhaps point out the difficulties in making any assessment

It is a good idea when tackling this kind of question to make the first sentence in each paragraph an analytical point before backing it up with factual evidence. For example, in paragraph one you could state that it was once thought that the enfranchisement of women would revolutionise women's political lives but this optimistic interpretation has recently been revised. You could then go on to demonstrate this with historical evidence. A useful way of doing this is to quote or paraphrase other historians. Do not be tempted just to tell the story but try to focus your material on the question set. The key to answering essay questions is relevance and analysis.

Summary Diagram

Conclusion: Life after Suffrage

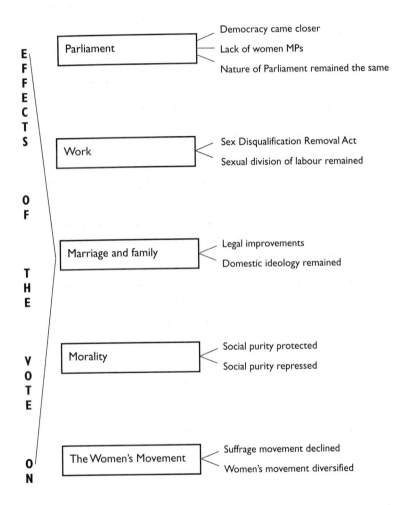

EFFECTS OF THE VOTE ON

Parliament
- Democracy came closer
- Lack of women MPs
- Nature of Parliament remained the same

Work
- Sex Disqualification Removal Act
- Sexual division of labour remained

Marriage and family
- Legal improvements
- Domestic ideology remained

Morality
- Social purity protected
- Social purity repressed

The Women's Movement
- Suffrage movement declined
- Women's movement diversified

Chronological Table

1832   Great Reform Act.
Henry Hunt introduced first petition in support of women's suffrage to Parliament.

1847   First leaflet on female suffrage by Anne Knight published.

1851   Sheffield Association for Female Franchise held its first meeting.

1865   Committee for Women's Suffrage formed in London.

1866   June, J.S. Mill presented women's suffrage to Parliament.
Women's Suffrage Provisional Committee formed.

1867   Second Reform Act.
Mill's amendment to include women in the Second Reform Bill defeated.
First permanent women's suffrage society founded in Manchester.

1868   National Society for Women's Suffrage (NSWS) founded.
Women's Suffrage Society founded in Birmingham, Bristol and Edinburgh.
Chorlton *v.* Lings case lost.

1866   First public meeting in London on votes for women held.

1870   Richard Pankhurst's women's suffrage Bill passed second reading.
Women's Suffrage Journal published.

1871   London National Society for Women's Suffrage founded.

1872   Central Committee of National Society for Women's Suffrage founded.

1877   New Central Committee of National Society for Women's Suffrage formed.

1881   Women granted the vote in the Isle of Man.

1884   Third Reform Act.

1888   Central National Committee of Women's Suffrage formed.
Central Committee of National Society for Women's Suffrage broke away.

1880   Women's Franchise League founded.

1892   Women's Emancipation League founded.

1897   National Union of Women's Suffrage Societies (NUWSS) founded.

1903   Women's Social and Political Union (WSPU) founded by Emmeline Pankhurst.
Lancashire and Cheshire Women Textile and Other Workers Representative Committee (LCWT) founded by Roper and Gore Booth.

1905   Christabel Pankhurst and Annie Kenney arrested for causing a disturbance.

1906   January, Liberals won landslide election.
Summer, WSPU moved to London.

1907   February, first Women's Parliament at Caxton Hall, London.

Women's Freedom League formed.
Votes for Women founded.
1908 February, Women's Suffrage Bill carried by 179 votes.
Women chained themselves to railings for the first time.
Beginning of organised heckling of Cabinet Ministers.
First window smashing.
1909 Second reading of Electoral Reform Bill which included votes for women.
Suffragettes banned from Liberal meetings.
First hunger strike and forcible feeding.
1910 July, Conciliation Bill carried by 139 votes in debate.
November 18th: Black Friday.
1911 Suffragettes resumed truce.
April, census boycotted.
May, Second Conciliation Bill debated.
June, Women's Coronation Procession of suffragettes and suffragists.
November, failure of Second Conciliation Bill results in resumption of violence by WSPU.
1912 Third Conciliation Bill failed second reading.
Christabel Pankhurst fled to France.
October, Pethick Lawrences left WSPU.
Suffragette newspaper founded by the Pankhursts.
Letter box damage began.
1913 Amendment to franchise bill ruled out of order by Speaker.
Lloyd George's country home firebombed; Golf greens ruined.
The Prisoner's Temporary Discharge for Ill Health Act (Cat and Mouse Act) passed.
June, death of Emily Davison sustained by injuries at Derby.
1914 February, ELFS split from the WSPU.
March, Mary Richardson slashed Rokeby Venus leading to closure of public galleries.
August, Britain declared war with Germany.
Suffragettes suspended militancy and joined war effort.
1915 Coalition Government formed.
1916 Lloyd George became Prime Minister.
Speaker's Conference set up
1918 February, Representation of the Peoples Act allowed women over 30 to vote.
Constance Markiewicz elected to Parliament but did not take her seat.
Nancy Astor became first women MP.
November, end of First World War.
1919 Sex Disqualification Act.
1920 Married Women's Property Act extended women's marital rights to property to Scotland.

1922 Married Women's Maintenance Act allowed women 40 shillings for herself and 10 shillings for each child.
Infanticide Act removed the charge of murder from women found guilty of infanticide.
Criminal Law Amendment Act removed the 'reasonable cause to believe' clause.

1923 Matrimonial Causes Act allowed wives equal grounds for divorce.
The Bastardy Act increased maintenance payments to single mothers.

1925 The Guardianship of Infants Act gave equal rights to men and women.
The Widows, Orphans and Old Age Contributory Pensions Act provided a pension and child allowances for widows of insured men.

1928 Representation of the People Act abolished the age qualification for women.

1969 Representation of the People Act gave vote to men and women over 18.

1997 116 women elected to Parliament.

Further Reading

A large number of books have been written on women's suffrage, so the list below merely offers a guide to the most accessible and important texts. Where a book has only been mentioned by author in the text, the full source details will be found below.

1 Primary Sources

Many of the autobiographical memoirs and histories written by suffragists have been reprinted allowing student access to valuable primary source material. Christabel Pankhurst's *Unshackled* (Hutchinson, 1959), Emmeline Pankhurst's *My Own Story* (Virago, 1979), Sylvia Pankhurst's *The Suffragette Movement* (Virago, 1977) and Ray Strachey's *The Cause* (Virago, 1978) are useful for student research projects because they were written by those actively engaged in the campaign for votes for women and provide insights into the minds of the important leaders of women's suffrage. For example in *My Own Story* the reader is made aware of Emmeline Pankhurst's enormous physical energy and emotional drive, as well as her developing political awareness. Nevertheless, autobiographies and histories written by those involved in the women's suffrage movement must be used with care. Emmeline Pankhurst's book was in fact written by an American journalist and contains many factual errors. Although Ray Strachey's book seems much more reasoned than that of Emmeline Pankhurst it must be remembered that she was a leading figure of the NUWSS and thus writes more favourably about them than the WSPU.

There are also useful primary source collections. Two of the most important are from the Women's Source Library. The first book, *Before the Vote was Won, Arguments for and against Women's Suffrasge 1864-1896* (Routledge and Kegan Paul, 1987), edited by Jane Lewis, traces the arguments mainly of those in support of women's suffrage, whereas the second, *Suffrage and the Pankhurst* (Routledge and Kegan Paul, 1987) edited by Jane Marcus, includes many useful articles, documents and pamphlets written by and about the Women's Social and Political Union. Both have interesting and thought-provoking introductions to the source material.

2 Secondary Sources

Until recently, the suffragettes have dominated the historiography of the struggle for votes for women. George Dangerfield's highly provocative *The Strange Death of Liberal England* (Perigree, 1980), which was first published in 1935, offers a scurrilously unsympathetic yet magnificently written account of the suffragette movement. To his credit, Dangerfield places the WSPU within the context of Edwardian England, so it is a useful book for those studying early twentieth century Britain as well as for those studying women's suffrage. For entertainment value alone Dangerfield is worth a read but those sympathetic to feminism might be offended by his interpretation. Unfortunately, much of Dangerfield's style has been reproduced by other historians who found it difficult to remain uninfluenced by his interpretative stance and style of writing. For example David Mitchell's equally readable *The Fighting Pankhursts* (Jonathan Cape, 1967) examines the WSPU leadership in some detail but trivialises the political motivation of the suffragette leaders. Similarly, Roger Fulford's *Votes for Women* (Faber and Faber, 1957), which recounts the wider story of the suffragists as well as the suffragettes, belittles their achievements. In contrast, Andrew Rosen's *Rise up Women* (Routledge and Kegan Paul, 1974) provides a scholarly narrative of the suffragette movement based on extensive research. This is a good analytical narrative of the suffragette movement which is well worth reading.

Some of the most important books to place women's suffrage within a wider political context are Constance Rover's *Women's Suffrage and Party Politics in Britain, 1866-1914* (Routledge and Kegan Paul, 1967), David Morgan's more specialist *Suffragists and Liberals* (Basil Blackwell, 1975), Martin Pugh's *Electoral Reform in War and Peace, 1906-1918* (Routledge and Kegan Paul, 1978) and Brian Harrison's *Separate Spheres* (Croom Helm, 1978). The first three of these books examine the relationship of the women's suffrage movement to the main political parties and to political reform, while the third analyses the opposition to women's suffrage. All four are excellent, scholarly works which, although written some time ago, do not demean women's struggle for the vote.

The birth and growth of feminist politics brought new interpretations of suffrage history. One of the first two historians to break both new empirical and methodological ground is Jill Liddington's and Jill Norris's *One Hand Tied Behind Us* (Virago, 1978). Liddington and Norris use local archives to construct an account of working-class suffragists active in the cotton towns of northern England. This book has done more than any other to break away from the belief that the suffrage movement was full of middle-class women. Yet, although Liddington and Norris have reinstated the suffragists in the story of votes for women, they are much too dismissive of the WSPU and tend to see the Pankhursts in a similar way as Dangerfield. Sandra Stanley Holton's *Feminism and Democracy* (Cambridge University Press, 1986), which also concentrates on the constitutionalist wing of the suffrage movement, offers a new perspective on suffrage history by placing the campaign for the vote within the wider framework of social reform politics.

On the other hand, American historians, who have a stronger tradition of radical feminism than British historians, tend to focus on a reappraisal of the WSPU. Recent feminist scholarship such as Martha Vicinus' *The Widening Sphere* (Methuen, 1972) portray suffragette militancy as a coherent response to the political situation because it challenged male authority. Indeed, there is a new trend within feminist historiography to place the suffrage movement within the context of sexual politics. Susan Kingsley Kent's *Sex and Suffrage in Britain, 1860-1914* (Routledge, 1987) suggests that women sought the vote in order to overturn the masculine social, economic and political order not as an end in itself.

Suffrage history, however, has concentrated on women: where men are mentioned it is in opposition to women's suffrage. The only book, so far, to examine men's support of women's suffrage is A.V. John's and Claire Eustance's edited *The Men's Share* (Routledge, 1997). This important book examines who these men were, the organisations they established and how they organised their support.

For those who enjoy reading biographies, Barbara Winslow's, *Sylvia Pankhurst* (UCL, 1996), B. Harrison's *Prudent Revolutionaries* (Clarendon Press, 1987) and Sandra Stanley Holton's *Suffrage Days, Stories from the Women's Suffrage Movement* (Routledge, 1996) are perhaps the most valuable because they place the story of the lives of suffrage activists within a political context.

Despite this increase in output on women's suffrage most books on the suffrage movement have concentrated on England. To redress this imbalance Leah Leneman's *A Guid Cause* (Aberdeen University Press, 1991) and Cliona Murphy's *The Women's Suffrage Movement and Irish Society in the Early Twentieth Century* (Harvester Wheatsheaf, 1989) examine the suffrage movement in Scotland and Ireland. They argue that whereas the suffrage movement in Scotland mirrored the English experience the Irish struggle for votes for women was uniquely different. In a seminal article by Catherine Hall "Rethinking Imperial Histories: The Reform Act of 1867" in *New Left Review* (1994) it is even argued that the British women's suffrage movement cannot be understood outside a global context of imperialism. Indeed, the British women's suffrage movement was part of a wider international suffrage movement which M. Nolan's and C. Daley's edited collection *Suffrage and Beyond, International Perspectives* (Auckland University Press, 1994) examines.

Of course, life did not end with the vote. Two useful books which evaluate women's achievements post-1918 are Joanna Alberti's *Beyond Suffrage* (Macmillan, 1989) and Martin Pugh's *Women and the Women's Movement in Britain, 1914-1959* (Macmillan, 1992).

Index

Acknowledgements

I would like to thank the series editor, Dr Robert Pearce, for the care he has taken in editing this book. His kind, yet rigorous, criticism has certainly made it much better. Thanks also to my colleagues in the History Division at the University of Wolverhampton for all their support, especially to Professor John Benson and Dr Fiona Terry-Chandler who made many helpful suggestions to improve the text and to Dr Malcolm Wanklyn for his encouragment throughout. Both Hilary Bourdillon and Ann Swarbrick helped with the study guides and student exercises, so I would like to thank them too. I am also grateful to the anonymous reader who made many useful detailed suggestions. My greatest thanks are to my husband, Jonathan Dudley, who commented on every chapter and whose support at every level has been much appreciated.

The publishers would like to thank the following for permission to reproduce the following copyright illustrations: Cover - reproduced courtesy of the London Museum. Punch Limited, p. 11; Mary Evans Picture Library, pp. 48 and 77; The British Library, p. 58; Imperial War Museum, p. 96.

The publishers would like to thank the following for permission to reproduce material in the volume:

Blackwell for an extract from *Suffragists and Liberals* by D. Morgan (1975) Cambridge University Press for the information which appeared on a map in *Votes for Women* by Di Atkinson (1988) and was used on the map on page 34 Clarendon Press for extracts from *Prudent Revolutionaries* by Brian Harrison (1987) and 'The Act of Militancy' in *Peaceable Kingdom, Stability and Change in Modern Britain* by Brian Harrison (1982); Croom Helm for extracts from *Separate Spheres: The Opposition to Women's Suffrage in Britain* by Brian Harrison (1978); Jonathan Cape for an extract from *Women This and Women That* by Lawrence Housman; Serif for extracts from *The Strange Death of Liberal England* by George Dangerfield (1980); Pandora for an extract from *Eva Gore Booth and Esther Roper* by Gifford Lewis (1988); Routledge and Kegan Paul for extracts from 'The Great Scourge and How to Fight it' by Christabel Pankhurst in S Jeffreys, *The Sexuality Debates* (1987), *Before the Vote was Won* by Jane Lewis (1987) and *Women's Suffrage and Party Politics in Britain, 1866-1914* by Constance Rover (1967); The Museum of London Suffrage Collection for extracts from *The Reformers' Year Book* by T.D. Benson and the Suffragette Testimonies; UCL for extracts from *Sylvia Pankhurst* by Barbara Winslow (1996); Virago Press for extracts from *My Own Story* by Emmeline Pankhurst (1979); *The Cause* by Ray Strachey (1978) and *Testament of Youth* by Vera Brittain (1992); and Wheatsheaf for an extract from *Women in England 1870-1950* by Jane Lewis (1984). The excerpt from *Testament of Youth* by Vera Brittain is included with the permission of her literary executors, and Victor Gollancz publishers.

Every effort has been made to trace and acknowledge ownership of copyright The publishers will be glad to make any suitable arrangements with copyright holders whom it has not been possible to contact.